TOTAL
KNITTING
fashions

Produced for Leisure Arts by MQ Publications Limited
MQ Publications New York office:
49 West 24th Street, 8th floor
New York, NY 10010
Phone: (+1) 212 223 6342
London office:
12 The Ivories
6–8 Northampton Street
London N1 2HY
Phone: + 44 (0)20 7359 2244
Website: www.mqpublications.com

Publisher and CEO: Zaro Weil
Group Sales Director: Simon Majumdar
Vice President of Sales and Marketing, North America: Stacey Ashton
Editorial Director: Ljiljana Baird
Editor: Sorrel Wood
Developmental Editor: BJ Berti
Technical Editor: Mari Lynn Patrick
Fashion Photography: Jennifer Lèvy
Hair and Make-up: Laly Zambrana
Steps Photography: Lizzie Orme
Design: Joanna Hill, Redbox Design

Made in the United States of America. First Printing.

International Standard Book Number 1-57486-582-X

TOTAL
KNITTING
fashions

MARI LYNN PATRICK

THE PROJECTS

introduction

My love of hand knitting design dates back to the mid 1960s when I was a teenager.
I fell in love with a photograph from a fashion magazine of a model wearing a hand knit
dress—she had a bouffant hairdo and was flying first class to Europe. Even in that
simple black and white photo, I remember the way the camera revealed the
sumptuousness of the hand knit stitches. Of course I had to knit that dress. To this day I
still think there are no other fashion shots as divine as those of hand knits. And I
continue to draw inspiration for my designs from great fashion photography.

In putting together this book I wanted to include designs that offer a wide variety of
styles to wear and smaller pieces to knit, while exposing both the first-time and more
experienced knitter to different ways of knitting. I thought about the projects in two
ways—as fashion pieces, and as techniques to inspire you to discover the pleasure of
learning a new skill or to take your skills to the next level.

My approach to the fashion aspect of knitting is to think of knits as accessories—even though many of the designs are wardrobe pieces like a coat, dress, and skirt. These garments can serve as fashion pieces in addition to embodying the functionality and coziness we associate with knitwear. Use them to accent and expand your wardrobe in a fresh, modern way.

My other driving interest is the technical aspect of knitting. I like to pay attention to the details of finishing and construction—and I design with that in mind. I hope this book will encourage pleasure in the aspects of knitting that I think about when creating designs. I find that I never get bored with knitting—it is a skill that you can continue to develop and expand on.

I hope that my passion for hand knitting and the designs in this book will inspire you to a similar love of knitting, and that it becomes for you, as for me, the affair of a lifetime. Enjoy!

black-lace cardigan

Edged in black lace trim, with a small velvet bow and covered buttons, this cardigan has a dramatically scooped neckline. The design makes use of the reverse side of the pattern stitch for added texture. You could choose to knit the cardigan in a different colorway, or change the ribbon trim to personalize the design.

SIZE
To fit Small (Medium, Large). Shown in size Medium. This is a standard fitting style.

FINISHED MEASUREMENTS
- Bust 34½ (36, 38)" / 87.5 (91.5, 96.5) cm
- Length 25½ (26, 26½)" / 65 (66, 67) cm
- Upper arm 12 (12½, 13)" / 30.5 (32, 33) cm

MATERIALS
  8 (8, 9) x 1¾ oz. (50 g) balls, each approx. 140 yd. (126 m) long, of Crystal Palace Yarns *Merino Frappe* (wool/nylon) in #145 Hibiscus
- Size 10 (6 mm) needles OR SIZE NECESSARY TO OBTAIN THE CORRECT GAUGE
- 6 yd. (5.5 m) of black stretch-lace trim (hem tape)
- ¼ yd. (23 cm) of ¼" (6 mm) wide velvet ribbon
- 5 x ⅞" (22 mm) buttons
- Small-eyed tapestry needle

GAUGE
19 sts and 29 rows = 4" (10 cm) over stamen st pat using size 10 (6 mm) needles. BE SURE TO CHECK THE GAUGE.

STAMEN STITCH PATTERN
Over an even number of sts.
Row 1 (RS) Knit.
Row 2 ★ K1, sl 1 purlwise wyib; rep from ★, ending k2.
Row 3 Knit.
Row 4 K2, ★ sl 1 purlwise wyib, k1; rep from ★ to end.
Rep row 1–4 for stamen st pat.

NOTE Sl sts are knit as alternating "floats" worked from the WS of the piece that show up on the RS of the piece. Before beg the WS row, always look at the RS of work to determine which pat row to work next.

Work all decs at edge of piece on the RS rows. Work all incs as M1 on the RS rows inside of the k1 selvage sts.

Cardigan

back

Cast on 82 (86, 90) sts. Work in stamen st pat dec 1 st each side every 16th row 4 times—74 (78, 82) sts. Work even until piece measures 11" (28 cm) from beg. Inc 1 st each side of next row then every 8th row 3 times more—82 (86, 90) sts. Work even until piece measures 17" (43 cm) from beg.

SHAPE ARMHOLES

Bind off 4 sts at beg of next 2 rows, 2 sts at beg of next 2 rows. Dec 1 st each side every other row 2 (3, 4) times—66 (68, 70) sts. Work even until armhole measures 7½ (8, 8½)" / 19 (20.5, 21.5) cm.

SHAPE NECK AND SHOULDER

Bind off 5 sts at beg of next 8 rows. Bind off center 26 (28, 30) sts for back neck.

left front

NOTE Read before beg to knit.

Cast on 46 (48, 50) sts. Work in stamen st pat dec 1 st at beg of RS rows (side seam edge) every 16th row 4 times—42 (44, 46) sts. Work even until piece measures 11" (28 cm) from beg. Inc 1 st at beg of next RS row (side seam edge) then rep inc every 8th row 3 times more, AT SAME TIME, when piece measures 15½ (16, 16½)" / 39.5 (40.5, 42) cm from beg, beg shaping neck as foll:

> **finishing tip** When applying stretch lace, trim slightly and miter the corners of the lace to fit. Do not cut the lace until you are finished with the trim to avoid working with small pieces.

SHAPE NECK

Next row (WS) Bind off 3 sts, work to end. Cont to shape neck, binding off 2 sts from neck edge 3 times more. Then dec 1 st from same edge every other row 3 (4, 5) times, and every 4th row 6 times, AT SAME TIME, when piece measures 17" (43 cm) from beg, shape armhole by binding off 4 sts from armhole edge once, then 2 sts once. Dec 1 st every other row 2 (3, 4) times—20 sts rem after all neck shaping is completed. Work even until armhole measures 7½ (8, 8½)" / 19 (20.5, 21.5) cm.

SHAPE SHOULDER

Bind off 5 sts from armhole edge 4 times.

right front

Place markers for 3 buttons on the left front, the first one at ¾" (2 cm) below the neck shaping, the others at 3" (7.5 cm) intervals. Work the right front to correspond to the left front, reversing all shaping and forming 3 buttonholes opposite markers at 4 sts from center edge by yo, k2tog for each buttonhole.

sleeves

Cast on 38 (40, 40) sts. Work in stamen st pat inc 1 st each side every 12th row 8 (8, 7) times, every 10th row 1 (1, 4) time(s)—56 (58, 62) sts. Work even until piece measures 18" (45.5 cm) from beg.

SHAPE CAP

Bind off 4 sts at beg of next 2 rows, then 2 sts at beg of next 2 rows. Dec 1 st each side every 2nd row twice, every 4th row 4 times, then every 2nd row 2 (3, 4) times. Bind off 3 sts at beg of next 6 rows.
Bind off rem 10 (10, 12) sts.

pocket flaps (make 2)

Cast on 26 sts. Work in stamen st pat for 6 rows. Dec 1 st each side on next (RS) row then every

other row twice more—20 sts. Work 1 row even. Bind off knitwise on RS.

finishing

Sew shoulder seams. Sew side and sleeve seams. Set in sleeves. Using the yarn, sew the lace trim (through the eyelet holes in the lace) to the lower edges of sleeves, pocket flaps, and around the neck, front, and lower edge of jacket. Sew pocket flaps on to cardigan, making sure they are symmetrical across the fronts. Sew on buttons to correspond with buttonholes. Make a small bow with ribbon and sew at the front V neck.

ribbon-tied bolero

Made in one piece with separate sleeves, this bolero is shaped to fit, and knit in reverse stockinette stitch. A dramatic fall of satin ribbon accentuates the yarn color and pulls through slits in the crochet-edge finishing.

SIZE

To fit Small (Medium, Large). Shown in size Small. This is a close fitting style.

FINISHED MEASUREMENTS

- Bust 32½ (34, 36)" / 82.5 (86, 91.5) cm
- Length 12 (13, 13¾)" / 30.5 (33, 35) cm
- Upper arm 12 (12½, 13)" / 30.5 (32, 33) cm

MATERIALS

 4 (5, 5) x 2 oz. (50 g) balls, each approx. 105 yd. (96 m) long, of Classic Elite Yarns *Calliope* (microfiber/viscose) in #5476 Harmony
- Size 7 (4.5 mm) needles OR SIZE NECESSARY TO OBTAIN CORRECT GAUGE
- Size 7 (4.5 mm) circular needle, 24" (60 cm) long
- Size 7 (4.5 mm) crochet hook
- 2 yd. (1.8 m) of 50 mm wide Mokuba double faced satin ribbon #1100 in #101 Turquoise

GAUGE

18 sts and 26 rows = 4" (10 cm) over reverse St st using size 7 (4.5 mm) needles. BE SURE TO CHECK THE GAUGE.

NOTE Bolero is worked in one piece to the armhole then separated for fronts and back at this point to work the armhole shaping.

Bolero

body

With circular needle, cast on 95 (103, 111) sts. Working in reverse St st (and work the first row as a knit row), work as foll:
Row 1 (WS) Knit.
Row 2 (RS) P1, inc 1 st in next st, p to last 2 sts, inc 1 st in next st, p1.
Row 3 (WS) K1, inc 1 st in next st, k to last 2 sts, inc 1 st in next st, k1.
[Rep the last 2 rows] 11 times more. Rep row 2 once more—145 (153, 161) sts. Work even until piece measures 4½ (4¾, 5)" / 11.5 (12, 12.5) cm from beg.

SEPARATE FOR ARMHOLES

Next row (RS) P30 (32, 34) (for right front), bind off next 8 sts, p next 69 (73, 77) sts (for back), bind off next 8 sts, p to end; the rem 30 (32, 34) sts are for left front. Leave the right front and back sts on hold on the circular needle and cont to work the left front sts only as foll:

left front

Working on the 30 (32, 34) left front sts only (and using the straight needles), bind off 2 sts from armhole edge once, dec 1 st every 2nd row 3 (4, 4) times—25 (26, 28) sts. Work even until armhole measures 2½ (3, 3½)" / 6.5 (7.5, 9) cm, ending with a WS row.

SHAPE NECK

Next (dec) row (RS) Purl to last 4 sts, p2tog, p2. Rep dec row every 4th row 6 times more—18 (19, 21) sts. Work even until armhole measures 6¾ (7½, 7¾)" / 17 (18.5, 19.5) cm.

SHAPE SHOULDER

From shoulder edge, bind off 6 sts 3 (2, 0) times, 7 sts 0 (1, 3) times.

back

Return to the 69 (73, 77) sts on hold for back and shape armholes by binding off 2 sts at beg of next 2 rows, dec 1 st each side every 2nd row 3 (4, 4) times—59 (61, 65) sts. Work even until armhole measures 6¾ (7¼, 7¾)" / 17 (18.5, 19.5) cm.

SHAPE SHOULDERS

Bind off 6 sts at beg of next 6 (4, 0) rows, 7 sts at beg of next 0 (2, 6) rows. Bind off rem 23 sts for back neck.

right front

Return to the 30 (32, 34) sts for right front and work as for left front, reversing shaping.

sleeves

With straight needles, cast on 46 (48, 50) sts. Working in reverse St st, inc 1 st each side of the 3rd row, then every 2nd row 3 times more—54 (56, 58) sts. Work even until piece measures 2" (5 cm) from beg.

SHAPE CAP

Bind off 4 sts at beg of next 2 rows, 2 sts at beg of next 2 rows. Dec 1 st each side every 2nd row 10 (11, 12) times, every 4th row twice. Bind off rem 18 sts.

finishing

Do not block pieces. Sew shoulder seams. Sew sleeve seams. Set in sleeves.

OUTER EDGE TRIM

With crochet hook, beg at back shoulder, work 24 sc across back neck, 20 (22, 24) sc along shaped left neck, 3 sc along the straight front edge, ch 3, skip 3 sts (for ribbon slit), 2 more sc along the straight front edge, 18 sc along the shaped front edge, 94 (102, 110) sc along the lower back edge, 18 sc along the shaped front edge, 2 sc along the straight front edge, ch 3, skip 3 sts (for ribbon slit), 3 sc along the straight front edge, 20 (22, 24) sc along the shaped right neck. Join and ch 2, turn. Working from WS, work 1 hdc in each sc and 3 hdc in the ch-3 loops. Fasten off.

SLEEVE CUFF TRIM

Working around the sleeve cuff with crochet hook, work 43 (45, 47) sc around each sleeve cuff. Fasten off.

RIBBON

Insert ribbon through slits formed by edging. Tie bow.

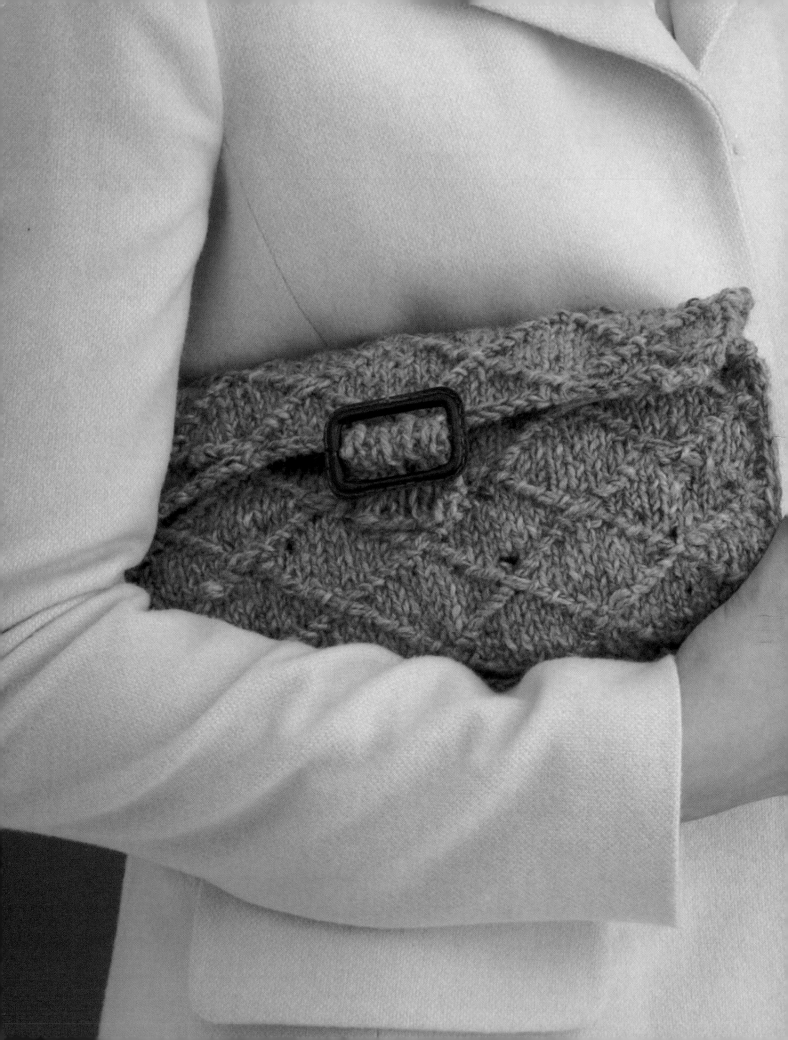

stitched tweed clutch

This rustic tweed clutch is worked in a quilt pattern stitch that is embroidered for extra definition. Sporting a decorative buckle flap closure and ribbed strap, the purse actually closes snugly with a magnetic snap under the flap. This purse would look good in any color—why not make one to match your favorite shoes?

FINISHED MEASUREMENTS

11" (28 cm) wide by 6" (15 cm) deep.

MATERIALS

 1 x 3½ oz. (100 g) hank approx. 183 yd. (167 m) long, of Tahki Stacy Charles *Homespun Donegal Tweed* (wool) in #834 Beige Tweed
- Size 7 (4.5 mm) needles OR SIZE NECESSARY TO OBTAIN CORRECT GAUGE
- Size H/8 (5 mm) crochet hook
- Tapestry needle
- Leather-bound weighted metal buckle, 2" (5 cm) wide by 1½" (4 cm) deep
- Magnetic snap closure

GAUGE

16 sts x 24 rows = 4" (10 cm) over quilted pat st using size 7 (4.5 mm) needles BE SURE TO CHECK THE GAUGE.

finishing tip Line inside of bag with stiff lining fabric, if desired, to help retain the square-edged shaping.

QUILTED PATTERN STITCH

Over a multiple of 10 sts plus 3 plus 2 selvage sts.
Row 1 (RS) K1 (selvage st), k1 ★ p1, k9★; rep between ★s, ending p1, k1, k1 (selvage st).
Row 2 K1 (selvage st), k1, p1, ★ k1, p7, k1, p1 ★; rep between ★s ending k1, k1 (selvage st).
Row 3 K1, k1, ★ k2, p1, k5, p1, k1 ★; rep between ★s, ending k2, k1.
Row 4 K1, p2, ★ p2, k1, p3, k1, p3 ★, rep between ★s, ending p1, k1.
Row 5 K1, k1, ★ k4, p1, k1, p1, k3 ★; rep between ★s, ending k2, k1.
Row 6 K1, p2, ★ p4, k1, p5 ★; rep between ★s, ending p1, k1.
Row 7 K1, k1, ★ k4, p1, k1, p1, k3 ★; rep between ★s, ending k2, k1.
Row 8 K1, p2, ★ p2, k1, p3, k1, p3 ★; rep between ★s, ending p1, k1.
Row 9 K1, k1, ★ k2, p1, k5, p1, k1 ★; rep between ★s, ending k2, k1.
Row 10 K1, p2, ★ k1, p7, k1, p1; rep between ★s, ending p1, k1.
Rep rows 1–10 for quilted pat st.

NOTE To familiarize yourself with the pattern st, cast on 25 sts and work the 10-row rep before beg to work the clutch instructions with shaping.

Clutch

back and flap

Cast on 35 sts.

Row 1 (RS) Work row 1 of quilted pat st, working rep 3 times.

Next (inc) row K1 into front and back of first st, work row 2 of pat st to last st, k1 into front and back of last st.

Rows 3-5 Rep the last (inc) row, working pat rows 3-5—43 sts. Work even until piece measures approx. 7" (18 cm) from beg, ending with pat row 7.

Dec row (RS) K1, skp, work pat to last 3 sts, k2tog, k1.

Dec row (WS) K1, p2tog, work pat to last 3 sts, p2tog tbl, k1.

Rep the last 2 rows once more. Bind off 35 sts.

front

Work as for back for 5" (12.5 cm). Bind off.

QUILTING

Using 2 strands of yarn and a tapestry needle, run yarn through the p-st bumps in the quilted design for extra dimension and raised effect.

finishing

Block pieces flat to measurements.

BUCKLE STRAP

Mark the center 9 sts on the RS of the front flap. Working into back loops only of these sts, pick up and k 9 sts in these sts from RS. Work in k1, p1 rib for 2" (5 cm). Bind off. Thread strap through a buckle and secure buckle in place at back. With crochet hook, from RS, join bag front and back tog, working in single crochet. Add magnetic snap closure under flap.

ribbon trim tank

Twisted knit ribs line up and then switch on the bodice of this shaped and fitted tank with a curved bustline front, worked in short rows. The narrow ribbon that threads through openings in the rib pattern adds a delicate finishing touch.

SIZE

To fit Small (Medium, Large). Shown in size Small. This is a close fitting style.

FINISHED MEASUREMENTS

- Bust 32 (34½, 37½)" / 81 (87.5, 95) cm
- Waist 27 (30, 33)" / 68.5 (76, 84) cm
- Length 20¾ (21¼, 21¾)" / 52.5 (54, 55) cm

MATERIALS

- 4 (5, 5) x 2½ oz. (70 g) balls, each approx. 168 yd.(154 m) long, of Lion Brand Yarns *Microspun* (microfiber acrylic) in #98 French Vanilla
- Size 5 (3.75 mm) needles OR SIZE NECESSARY TO OBTAIN CORRECT GAUGE
- Size 4 (3.5 mm) circular needle, 24" (60 cm) long
- 2 yd. (1.8 m) of 5 mm wide Mokuba ribbon #4671 in #12 Burgundy

GAUGE

22 sts and 30 rows = 4" (10 cm) over St st using size 5 (3.75 mm) needles. BE SURE TO CHECK THE GAUGE.

STITCH GLOSSARY

K1tbl K1 through back loop.

NOTE Back and front are the same except for short-row shaping under the front bust line that begins the ribbed yoke pattern.

Tank

back

With size 5 (3.75 mm) needles, cast on 83 (91, 99) sts.

Row 1 (RS) P1, ★ k1tbl, p3; rep from ★, ending k1tbl, p1.

Row 2 K1, ★ p1, k3; rep from ★ ending p1, k1. Rep these 2 rows for rib until there are 8 rows in rib. Then, beg with a k row, work in St st dec 1 st each side every 10th row 3 times—77 (85, 93) sts. Work even until piece measures 7" (18 cm) from beg. Inc 1 st each side of next row then every 6th row twice more—83 (91, 99) sts. Work even until piece measures 10" (25.5 cm) from beg.

★★ FIRST RIB PATTERN

Row 1 (RS) P1, ★ sl 1 knitwise wyib, p7; rep from ★, ending sl 1 knitwise wyib, p1.

Row 2 K1, ★ sl 1 purlwise wyif, k7; rep from ★ ending sl 1 purlwise wyif, k1.

NOTE These first 2 rows comprise the sl sts that will form the drawstring row for the ribbon.

Row 3 (RS) P1, ★ k1tbl, p7; rep from ★, ending k1tbl, p1.

Row 4 K1, ★ p1, k7; rep from ★, ending p1, k1. Rep rows 3 and 4 for yoke rib pat, AT SAME TIME, inc 1 st each end of next RS row then every 6th row twice more—89 (97, 105) sts. Work even in yoke rib pat until piece measures 13" (33 cm) from beg.

SHAPE ARMHOLES

Bind off 5 (5, 6) sts at beg of next 2 rows, then 2 sts at beg of next 2 (2, 4) rows. Dec 1 st each side every other row 6 (8, 8) times—63 (67, 69) sts. Work even until armhole measures 2¾ (3¼, 3¾)" / 7 (8, 9.5) cm.

SECOND RIB PATTERN

Next row (RS) P3 (1, 6), ★ k1tbl, p7; rep from ★, ending last rep p3 (1, 6). The new rib pat is now set up with k1 ribs in the center of each p7 rib. This rib will cont to end of piece. Work 1 row even. Inc 1 st each side of next row then every 4th row 6 times more, AT SAME TIME, when armhole measures 5¼ (5¾, 6¼)" / 13.5 (14.5, 16) cm, work the neck shaping as foll:

---

short row wrapping (wrap and turn—w & t)

KNIT SIDE

1) Wyib, sl next st purlwise.

2) Move yarn between the needles to the front.

3) Sl the same st back to LH needle. Turn work, bring yarn to the p side between needles. One st is wrapped. When short rows are completed, work to just before wrapped st, insert RH needle under the wrap and knitwise into the wrapped st and k them tog.

PURL SIDE

1) Wyif, sl next st purlwise.

2) Move yarn between the needles to the back of work.

3) Sl same st back to LH needle. Turn work, bring yarn back to the p side between the needles. One st is wrapped. When short rows are completed, work to just before wrapped st, insert RH needle from behind into the back lp of the wrap and place on LH needle; p wrap tog with st on needle.

turn (or to last 13 sts), w & t.

Short row 4 Work to 3 sts before last short row turn (or to last 13 sts), w & t.

Short rows 5–16 Rep short rows 3 and 4, always working 3 sts less on each short row that is:

Short row 5 To last 16 sts.

Short row 6 To last 16 sts.

Short row 7 To last 19 sts.

Short row 8 To last 19 sts.

Short row 9 To last 22 sts.

Short row 10 To last 22 sts.

Short row 11 To last 25 sts.

Short row 12 To last 25 sts.

Short row 13 To last 28 sts.

Short row 14 To last 28 sts.

Short row 15 To last 31 sts.

Short row 16 To last 31 sts.

Next 2 rows Work even to end of each row, closing up the holes made by the wrapped sts (see short row wrapping opposite).

Piece should measure 10" (25.5 cm) from beg. Find this point, ★★ First Rib Pattern on back, and work and complete as for back.

finishing

Do not block pieces.

ARMHOLE TRIM

Pick up and k 39 (43, 47) sts from back armhole, cast on 4 sts, pick up and k 39 (43, 47) sts from front armhole—82 (90, 98) sts. Work in k1, p1 rib for 2 rows. Bind off in rib. Rep for other armhole.

NECK TRIM

Pick up and k 160 (166, 170) sts around neck edge. Work in k1, p1 rib for 2 rows. Bind off in rib. Sew side seams.

RIBBON

Draw ribbon through the ss ribs and tie in bow.

SHAPE NECK

Next row (RS) Work to center 39 (43, 45) sts, join a 2nd ball of yarn and bind off these center 39 (43, 45) sts, work to end.

Cont to shape neck (and cont with the side armhole incs) binding off 4 sts from each neck edge 4 times, 3 sts once.

front

Work as for back until piece measures 9¾" (24.5 cm) from beg.

SHORT ROW SHAPING

Short row 1 (RS) Work to last 10 sts, wrap and turn (w & t).

Short row 2 Work to last 10 sts, w & t.

Short row 3 Work to 3 sts before last short row

mini ribbed
vest and cuffs

Tiny ribs knit in a double strand of yarn with distinctive stretchability work really well in this tiny vest with matching ribbed cuffs. Trimmed with a pale contrast color, the set would look just as good worked all in one color, or with the contrast reversed—choose buttons that blend with the trim color to keep the style.

SIZE

To fit Small (Medium, Large). Shown in size Medium. This is a close-fitting style.

FINISHED MEASUREMENTS

- Bust (closed) 32 (34, 36)" / 81 (86, 91.5) cm
- Length 13 (13½, 14)" / 33 (34, 35.5) cm
- Cuff is 4½" (11.5cm) long; 7½" (19 cm) around

MATERIALS

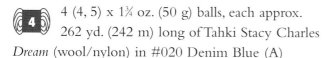

- 4 (4, 5) x 1¾ oz. (50 g) balls, each approx. 262 yd. (242 m) long of Tahki Stacy Charles *Dream* (wool/nylon) in #020 Denim Blue (A)
- 2 x 1¾ oz. (50 g) balls, each approx. 262 yd. (242 m) long, of Tahki Stacy Charles *Dream* (wool/nylon) in #02 Ecru (B)
- Size 6 (4 mm) and 7 (4.5 mm) needles OR SIZE NECESSARY TO OBTAIN CORRECT GAUGE
- 9 x ½" (1.2 cm) buttons

GAUGE

VEST

26 sts and 26 rows = 4" (10 cm) over k1, p2 rib using 2 strands of yarn, and larger needles.

CUFFS

28 sts and 28 rows = 4" (10 cm) over k1, p2 rib using 2 strands of yarn and smaller needles. BE SURE TO CHECK THE GAUGE.

NOTE Work with 2 strands of yarn held tog throughout.

Vest

back

With smaller needles and 2 strands of A, cast on 92 (98, 104) sts.

Row 1 (RS) P2, ★ k1, p2; rep from ★ to end. Cont in k1, p2 rib for 3 rows more. Change to larger needles and inc 1 st each side every 4th row 6 times—104 (110, 116) sts. Work even until piece measures 5" (12.5 cm) from beg.

SHAPE ARMHOLES

NOTE Read before beg to knit.
Bind off 4 sts at beg of next 2 rows, 2 sts at beg of next 6 rows. Dec 1 st each side every 2nd row 2 (3, 4) times—80 (84, 88) sts. Work even until armhole measures 2½ (3, 3½)" / 6.5 (7.5, 9) cm. Inc 1 st each side of next row, then every 4th row 5 times more—92 (96, 100) sts, AT SAME TIME, when armhole measures 5½ (6, 6½)" / 14 (15, 16.5) cm, shape back neck by binding off center 38 sts and working both sides at once, bind off 3 sts from each neck edge 3 times, 2 sts once, AT SAME TIME, when armhole measures 6½ (7, 7½)" / 16.5 (18, 19) cm, shape shoulders by binding off from each shoulder edge 3 sts 4 (3, 0) times, 4 (5, 4) sts 1 (2, 5) times.

left front

With smaller needles and 2 strands of A, cast on 44 (47, 50) sts. Work in k1, p2 rib as on back for 4 rows. Change to larger needles and inc 1 st at armhole edge (beg of RS rows) every 4th row 6 times, AT SAME TIME, when piece measures 3½ (3½, 4)" / 9 (9, 10) cm from beg, ending with a RS row and shape neck as foll:

SHAPE NECK

Next row (WS) Bind off 9 sts, work to end. Cont to shape neck, binding off 3 sts from neck edge once, 2 sts twice, then dec 1 st [k2tog, p1 at end of RS rows] every 2nd row 10 times, then every 4th row twice, AT SAME TIME, when piece measures 5" (12.5 cm) from beg, shape armhole by binding off 4 sts from armhole edge once, 2 sts 3 times, dec 1 st every 2nd row 2 (3, 4) times. Then, when armhole measures 2½ (3, 3½)" / 6.5 (7.5, 9) cm, inc 1 st at armhole edge on next row, then every 4th row 5 times more. There are 16 (18, 20) sts after all shaping is completed. When armhole measures 6½ (7, 7½)" / 16.5 (18, 19) cm, shape shoulder same as on back.

right front

Work as for left front, reversing all shaping.

finishing

Do not block or press pieces. Sew shoulder seams.

ARMHOLE TRIM

With smaller needles and 2 strands B, pick up and
k 63 (68, 73) sts around armholes. P2 rows. K1 row.
Bind off purlwise. Sew side seams.

LEFT FRONT TRIM

With smaller needles and 2 strands of A, pick up
and k 19 (19, 21) sts along left front edge. Bind
off knitwise.

RIGHT FRONT TRIM

With smaller needles and 2 strands of B, pick up
and k 19 (19, 21) sts along right front edge.

BUTTONHOLE ROW (WS)

P2, ★ p2tog, yo, p4 (4, 5); rep from ★ once, yo,
p2tog, p3. P1 row. K1 row. Bind off purlwise.

NECKLINE TRIM

With smaller needles and 2 strands of B, pick up
and k 56 sts from right front neck edge, 54 sts
around back neck (picking up 1 st in each k st
and 1 st in each p2 rib), 56 sts from left front
edge. Work as for armhole trim. Sew on buttons to
left front trim.

Cuffs (make 2)

With smaller needles and 2 strands of A, cast on
44 sts.

Row 1 (RS) ★ P2, k1; rep from ★, ending p2.
Work in rib as established for 4" (10 cm). Bind off.

LEFT SIDE TRIM

With smaller needles and 2 strands A, pick up and
k 19 sts along one side edge. Bind off knitwise.

RIGHT SIDE TRIM

On opposite side edge, with smaller needles and 2
strands B, pick up and k 21 sts.

BUTTONHOLE ROW (WS)

P1, [p2tog, yo, p6] twice, p2tog, yo, p2. P1 row.
K1 row. Bind off knitwise.

LOWER EDGE TRIM

With smaller needles and 2 strands B, pick up and
k 40 sts along lower edge of cuff. P2 rows. K1 row.
Bind off knitwise. Sew buttons on to left side cuff.

fashion tip For a longer vest, increase
the length as desired before beginning the
armholes, by adding more rows between
each side increase.

tank top **dress**

A-line dress that falls below the knees, with inset flares at the hem and bustline detail shaping is knit in a dense but light-weight shimmery yarn. It can be dressed up or down depending on the accessories chosen. Here, a simple ribbon belt slims the waistline while pearls add a classic touch.

SIZE
To fit Small (Medium, Large). Shown in size Medium. This is a standard fitting style with stretchable fit.

FINISHED MEASUREMENTS
- Bust 30 (32, 34)" / 76 (81, 86) cm
- Length 39 (40, 41)" / 99 (101.5, 104) cm

MATERIALS
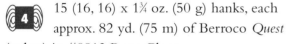 15 (16, 16) x 1¾ oz. (50 g) hanks, each approx. 82 yd. (75 m) of Berroco *Quest* (nylon) in #9813 Rose Glow
- Size 9 (5.5 mm) needles OR SIZE NECESSARY TO OBTAIN CORRECT GAUGE
- Stitch markers

GAUGE
19 sts and 26 rows = 4" (10 cm) over St st using size 9 (5.5 mm) needles. BE SURE TO CHECK THE GAUGE.

Dress

back
With size 9 (5.5 mm) needles, cast on 155 (160, 165) sts.
Row 1 (WS) K33 (35, 37), pm (place marker), k29, pm, k31 (32, 33), pm, k29, pm, k33 (35, 37).
Flare dec row (RS) K to first marker, sl marker and skp, k to 2 sts before next marker, k2tog, sl marker (for first flare), k to 3rd marker, sl marker and skp, k to 2 sts before next marker, k2tog, k to end.
Next row Purl.
Rep last 2 rows 12 times more. There are 3 sts between each set of markers.
Next row (RS) K to first set of markers, remove markers and skp between markers, k to 2nd set of markers and remove markers and skp between markers, k to end—101 (106, 111) sts. P1 row.
Next (side dec) row (RS) K1, skp, k to last 3 sts, k2tog, k1.
Rep side dec row every 8th row 6 times more, every 6th row 9 times—69 (74, 79) sts. Piece measures approx. 20" (50 cm) from beg. Then, rep side dec row every 6th row 4 (5, 6) times more—61 (64, 67) sts. Work even for 3" (7.5 cm) or 19 rows more. Adjust length, if desired at this point.

Inc row (RS) K2, inc 1 st in next st, k to last 3 sts, inc 1 st in next st, k2. Rep inc row every 6th row 4 times more—71 (74, 77) sts.
Work even until piece measures 31½ (32½, 33½)" / 80 (82.5, 85) cm from beg.

SHAPE ARMHOLES

Bind off 2 (3, 3) sts at beg of next 2 rows.
Dec row 1 (RS) K2, p1, skp, k to last 5 sts, k2tog, p1, k2.
Dec row 2 (WS) P2, k1, p2tog, p to last 5 sts, p2tog tbl (through back loop), k1, p2. Rep last 2 rows once more.
[Rep dec row 1. Work 1 row even] twice—55 (56, 59) sts. On Medium size only, dec 1 st at center of next row for 55 sts. Work even (keeping 3-st detail at armholes) until armhole measures 3" (7.5 cm), ending with a RS row.

SHAPE NECK

Next row (WS) Work 23 (23, 25) sts, k1, p2, k3, p2, k1 (for center 9 sts), work to end.
Dec row (RS) Work to 2 sts before center 9 sts, k2tog, p1, k2, join 2nd ball of yarn and bind off 3 sts purlwise, k2, p1, skp, work to end.
Dec 1 st at neck edge every row (on the WS rows, working p2tog on first dec and p2tog tbl on 2nd) until 7 sts rem each side. Work even until armhole measures 6 (6, 6½)" / 15 (15, 16.5) cm. Bind off sts each side for shoulders.

> **fashion tip** Use a ribbon tie as shown for a blouson look at the hips, or tie ribbon just below the bust to get an empire effect.

front

Work as for back, including the flares and side shaping, until piece measures 3¼" (8 cm) below the armhole shaping.

SHAPE BUST

NOTE Read before cont to knit, because the interior bust shaping will take place along with the neck and armhole shaping.
Bust (inc) row (RS) Work to center 27 (27, 29) sts, M1, pm, k 27 (27, 29) pm, M1, work to end.
Rep bust inc row (working M1 before first marker and M1 after 2nd marker) every other row 7 times more. Work 3 rows even.
Bust (dec) row (RS) Work 2 sts before first marker, skp, work to 2nd marker, k2tog, work to end.
Rep bust dec row every other row 7 times more, AT SAME TIME, shape armhole as on back. When same length as back and when there is 1" (2.5 cm) in armhole, work neck shaping simultaneously beg on RS row as foll:
Next row (WS) Work to center 7 sts, k1, p2, k1, p2, k1, work to end.
Dec row (RS) Work to 2 sts before center 7 sts, k2tog, p1, k2, join 2nd ball of yarn and bind off 1 st purlwise, k2, p1, skp, work to end. Cont with bust shaping, dec 1 st at each neck edge every row until 7 sts rem each side. Work even until armhole measures same as back. Bind off rem 7 sts each side for shoulders.

finishing

Do not block pieces. Sew shoulder and side seams.

simple shawl collar cardigan

Luxurious yet practical, this cardigan with an extra wide shawl collar can be worn open or closed with a decorative pin. It will work either dressed up—as shown—or provide pizzazz to a simple T-shirt and jeans combination. This classic cardigan will take you through the day, and still look great in the evening.

SIZE

To fit Small (Medium, Large). Shown in size Small. This is a standard fitting style.

FINISHED MEASUREMENTS

- Bust (closed) 35 (37, 39½)" / 89 (94, 100) cm
- Length 23¾ (24¼, 24¾)" / 60 (61.5, 63) cm
- Upper arm 13½ (14½, 15¾)" / 34 (37, 40) cm

MATERIALS

 13 (14, 15) x 1¾ oz. (50 g) balls, each approx. 110 yd. (100.5 m) long, of Skacel Collection *Drama* (polyamide) in #10340 Purple Mix
- Size 8 (5 mm) and 10 (6 mm) needles OR SIZE NECESSARY TO OBTAIN CORRECT GAUGE

GAUGE

14 sts and 24 rows = 4" (10 cm) over St st using larger needles. BE SURE TO CHECK THE GAUGE.

Cardigan

back

With smaller needles, cast on 63 (67, 71) sts. Work in k1, p1 rib for 2¼" (6 cm). Change to larger needles and work in St st, dec 1 st each side every 6th row 3 times, every 4th row 4 times—49 (53, 57) sts. Work even until piece measures 10¾" (27 cm) from beg.

Inc row (RS) Inc 1 st each side of row. Rep inc row every 6th row twice more, every 4th row 3 times more—61 (65, 69) sts. Work even until piece measures 15¾" (40 cm) from beg.

SHAPE ARMHOLES

Bind off 3 sts at beg of next 2 rows, 2 sts at beg of next 2 rows, and then 1 st at beg of next 2 (4, 6) rows—49 (51, 53) sts. Work even until armhole measures 7 (7½, 8)" / 18 (19, 20.5) cm.

SHAPE SHOULDERS

Bind off 4 sts at beg of next 2 (4, 4) 2 rows, 3 sts at beg of next 4 (2, 2) rows—29 (29, 31) sts. Bind off. Place a yarn marker at center back neck.

right front

NOTE Read before beg to knit.

With smaller needles, cast on 46 (48, 50) sts. Work in k1, p1 rib for 2¼" (6 cm). Change to larger needles.

Row 1 (RS) Cast on 5 sts (for front facing), k to end—51 (53, 55) sts.

Cont in St st, dec'ing at end of RS rows every 6th row 3 times, then every 4th row 4 times. When piece measures 10¾" (27 cm), inc 1 st at seam edge (end of RS row) on this row then every 6th row twice more, every 4th row 3 times, AT SAME TIME, beg to inc for the front facing when piece measures 5" (12.5 cm) above the band—or 7¼" (18.5 cm) from beg—by inc 1 st at beg of the next RS row then every 2nd row 11 times, every 4th row 12 times. When piece measures same as back to armhole, shape armhole as on back by binding off at beg of WS rows, 3 sts once, 2 sts once and 1 st 1 (2, 3) times—68 (69, 70) sts rem—10 sts are the shoulder, 58 (58, 59) sts are the collar and facing. Work even until armhole measures 7 (7½, 8)" / 18 (19, 20.5) cm.

SHAPE SHOULDER

From shoulder edge (beg of WS rows), bind off 4 sts 1 (2, 2) time(s), 3 sts 2 (1, 1) time(s)—58 (58, 59) sts. Sl sts to a holder to work the collar later.

left front

Work as for right front, reversing all shaping.

sleeves

With smaller needles, cast on 29 (31, 31) sts. Work in k1, p1 rib for 2¼" (6 cm). Change to larger needles and cont in St st inc 1 st each side every 8th (8th, 6th) row 9 (10, 12) times—47 (51, 55) sts. Work even until piece measures 17½" (44.5 cm) from beg.

SHAPE CAP

Bind off 3 sts at beg of next 2 rows, then 2 sts at beg of next 2 rows. Dec 1 st each side every other row 6 (8, 10) times, every 4th row 3 times. Bind off 2 sts at beg of next 4 rows. Bind off rem 11 sts.

finishing

Do not block pieces. Sew shoulder seams.

COLLAR EXTENSION

Return to the 58 (58, 59) sts from right front collar and facing and cont in St st for approx. 4" (10 cm), or until the side edge fits into the center back neck marker. Work left front collar in same way. Using the 3-needle bind-off method (see page 40), join collar at center back neck. Sew collar to back neck. Fold the 5-st facing to the purl side and sew neatly in place. Sew side and sleeve seams. Set in sleeves.

chunky aran hat

One ball of super chunky yarn makes this easy cabled hat fast to knit—an ideal weekend project. The amusing topknot is made with two lengths of simple crocheted cord attached to the crown. To finish, just make a simple knot on the end of each cord and tie them together in a loose knot.

FINISHED MEASUREMENTS

- Head circumference 21" (53 cm)
- Depth 7" (18 cm)

MATERIALS

5 1 x 5 oz. (140 g) ball approx. 153 yd. (140 m) long, of Lion Brand Yarn *Wool-Ease Chunky* (acrylic/wool) in #133 Pumpkin
- Set (5) of double-pointed needles (dpn) size 10½ (6.5 mm) OR SIZE NECESSARY TO OBTAIN CORRECT GAUGE
- Cable needle (cn)
- Size I/9 (5.5 mm) crochet hook
- Stitch markers

GAUGE

16 rib sts and 16 rows/rnds = 4" (10 cm) over k2, p2 rib using size 10½ (6.5 mm) needles. BE SURE TO CHECK THE GAUGE.

STITCH GLOSSARY

3-st RPC Sl 1 st to cn and hold to back, k2, p1 from cn.
3-st LPC Sl 2 sts to cn and hold to front, p1, k2 from cn.
6-st RC Sl 3 sts to cn and hold to back, k3, k3 from cn.

CENTER CABLE PATTERN

Worked in rnds over 22 sts.
Set-up rnd 1 P5, k2, p1, k6, p1, k2, p5.
Rnd 2 P4, 3-st RPC, p1, k6, p1, 3-st LPC, p4.
Rnd 3 P3, 3-st RPC, p2, k6, p2, 3-st LPC, p3.
Rnd 4 P2, 3-st RPC, p3, k6, p3, 3-st LPC, p2.
Rnd 5 P1, 3-st RPC, p4, 6-st RC, p4, 3-st LPC, p1.
Rnd 6 P1, k2, p5, k6, p5, k2, p1.
Rnd 7 P1, 3-st LPC, p4, k6, p4, 3-st RPC, p1.
Rnd 8 P2, 3-st LPC, p3, k6, p3, 3-st RPC, p2.
Rnd 9 P3, 3-st LPC, p2, k6, p2, 3-st RPC, p3.
Rnd 10 P4, 3-st LPC, p1, k6, p1, 3-st RPC, p4.
Rnd 11 P5, k2, p1, 6-st RC, p1, k2, p5.
Rep rnds 2-11 (10 row repeat) for central cable pat.

3-Needle bind-off With the RS of pieces tog and the needles parallel, insert a 3rd needle into the first st from front needle and first st from back needle and k them tog. Rep with the next 2 sts. Sl the first st on the 3rd needle over the 2nd st and off the needle. Rep until all sts are joined and bound off.

Hat

Cast on 68 sts and divide evenly with 17 sts on each of 4 dpn. Join and pm to mark beg of rnds.

Rnd 1 Purl.

Rnd 2 Knit.

Rnd 3 K into front and back of next 2 sts, p2, k2 ★, pm, p5, [k2, p into front and back of next st] 4 times, k2, p5, pm ★, k2, p2, k into front and back of each of next 2 sts, p2, k2, rep between ★s once, k2, p2—80 sts. Cont to work hat in this way, working the 2 sets of 22 sts between markers in central cable pat and the 18 sts between these sections in k2, p2 rib as established, until 20 more rows have been worked in pat (or desired depth of hat) and on last rnd, place new markers to mark the central k2 cable in the k2, p2 rib at each side (or rib 8 sts, pm, rib 2, pm, rib 8 sts in each set of ribs).

Dec rnd ★ Work to 3 sts before the new (rib) marker, sk2p, k2, k3tog; rep from ★ once more, work to end of rnd.

Rep dec rnd every rnd 6 times more—24 sts.

finishing

Divide the 24 sts evenly onto 2 needles (12 sts on each needle) and turn the hat to WS to finish. Using the 3-needle bind-off method (see opposite), join the top of hat tog.

TOGGLE CLOSURE

With crochet hook, join yarn to top of one cable and ch 38, turn, Sl st in each ch and join to top of hat and fasten off. Make a 2nd toggle chain as first on the opposite side of the cable. Double knot at top and knot ends of chains.

camel coat

Shaped three-quarter length coat with contrast striped trims in garter stitch. The coat

has a collar and button-trimmed wraparound belt at the back, waist shaping, and

slight flare at the hem for added panache. A rose corsage adds a feminine flourish.

SIZE

To fit Small (Medium, Large). Shown in size Small. This is a standard fitting style.

FINISHED MEASUREMENTS

- Lower edge 49 (51, 53)" / 125 (129, 134) cm
- Bust (buttoned) 37 (39, 41)" / 94 (99, 104) cm
- Length 34 (35, 36)" / 86 (89, 91.5) cm
- Upper arm 13 (13½, 14¼)" / 33 (34, 36) cm

MATERIALS

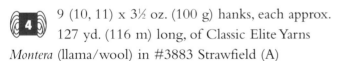 9 (10, 11) x 3½ oz. (100 g) hanks, each approx. 127 yd. (116 m) long, of Classic Elite Yarns *Montera* (llama/wool) in #3883 Strawfield (A)
- 1 x 3½ oz. (100 g) hank approx. 127 yd. (116 m) long, of Classic Elite Yarns *Montera* (llama/wool) #3882 Bold Rose (B)
- Size 9 (5.5 mm) needles OR SIZE NECESSARY TO OBTAIN CORRECT GAUGE
- Size 7 (4.5 mm) circular needle, 24" (60 cm) long for the front trims
- Size 7 (4.5 mm) needles for back ribbed waistband
- 6 x 1¼" (3 cm) buttons

GAUGE

16 sts and 22 rows = 4" (10 cm) over St st using size 9 (5.5 mm) needles. BE SURE TO CHECK THE GAUGE.

NOTE Work a k1 selvage st at beg and end of each row.

Coat

back

With size 9 (5.5 mm) needles and A, cast on 98 (102, 106) sts. K4 rows. Change to B and k4 rows. Then, beg with a k row, and cont with A, work in St st (keeping 1 k st at beg and end of each row in garter st) for 6 rows more.

Dec row (RS) K2, skp, k to last 4 sts, k2tog, k2. Rep dec row every 8th row twice more, every 6th row 8 times, every 4th row 6 times—64 (68, 72) sts. Change to size 7 (4.5 mm) needles and work in k1, p1 rib (for back waistband) for 2" (5 cm). Change back to size 9 (5.5 mm) needles.

Next (inc) row (RS) K1, inc 1 st in next st, k to last 3 sts, inc 1 st in next st, k2. Rep inc row every 6th row 4 times more—74 (78, 82) sts.

Work even until piece measures 25 (25½, 26)" / 63.5 (65, 66) cm from beg; (OR 6 (6½, 7)" / 15 (16.5, 18) cm above waistband).

SHAPE ARMHOLES

Bind off 4 sts at beg of next 2 rows, 2 sts at beg of next 2 rows.

Dec row (RS) k2, skp, k to last 4 sts, k2tog, k2. Rep dec row every 2nd row 2 (3, 4) times more—56 (58, 60) sts. Work even until armhole measures 7½ (8, 8½)" / 19 (20.5, 21.5) cm.

SHAPE NECK AND SHOULDERS

Bind off 4 sts at beg of next 4 (4, 6) rows, and 3 sts at beg of next 6 (6, 4) rows, AT SAME TIME as the 5th shoulder bind-off, bind off center 18 (20, 20) sts for neck and working both sides at once, bind off 2 sts from each neck edge once.

left front

With size 9 (5.5 mm) needles and A, cast on 49 (51, 53) sts. Work 8 rows in garter st as for back. Then cont in St st for 6 rows.

Dec row (RS) K2, skp, k to end. Rep dec row every 8th row twice more, every 6th row 8 times, every 4th row 6 times—32 (34, 36) sts.

NOTE The front at the waist is worked in St st, not in k1, p1 rib as on the back.

Work even in St st for 2" (5 cm).

Next (inc) row (RS) K1, inc 1 st in next st, k to end. Rep inc row every 6th row 4 times more—37 (39, 41) sts. Work even until piece measures same length as back to armhole.

SHAPE ARMHOLE

Bind off 4 sts at beg of next (RS) row then bind off 2 sts from same edge once more.

> **finishing tip** Be sure to bind off the center front and all trim edges firmly so that pieces will lie flat.

Dec row (RS) K2, skp, k to end.
Rep dec row every other row 2 (3, 4) times more—28 (29, 30) sts. Work even until armhole measures 5 (5½, 6)" / 12.5 (14, 15) cm with a RS row.

SHAPE NECK

Next row (WS) Bind off 3 (4, 5) sts, work to end. Cont to shape neck, binding off 2 sts from neck edge 4 times more—17 (17, 18) sts. When armhole measures same as back, shape shoulder as on back.

right front

Work as for left front, reversing shaping.

sleeves

With size 9 (5.5 mm) needles and A, cast on 40 (42, 43) sts. Work 8 rows in garter st as for back. Then cont with A only in St st inc 1 st each side every 12th row 6 (6, 7) times—52 (54, 57) sts. Work even until piece measures 18" (45.5 cm) from beg.

CAP SHAPING

Bind off 4 sts at beg of next 2 rows, 2 sts at beg of next 2 rows. Dec 1 st each side every 2nd row 9 (10, 11) times, every 4th row once. Bind off 2 sts at beg of next 4 rows. Bind off 12 (12, 13) sts.

back belt

With size 9 (5.5 mm) needles and B, cast on 82 (84, 86) sts. K4 rows. With A, [k1 row, p1 row] 3 times (for 6 rows in St st). With B, k4 rows. Bind off.

SIDE TRIM ON BELT

With size 9 (5.5 mm) needles and B, pick up and k 11 sts along one side of belt. K3 rows. Bind off. Rep on the other side.

LEFT AND RIGHT FRONT TRIM

With circular needle, pick up and k 119 (123, 127) sts along left front edge with B, then the last 4 sts (to match lower border) with A. K3 rows. Cut B and with A only, k4 rows. Bind off. Place markers for 4 buttons, the first one at 14" (36 cm) from lower edge and the others evenly spaced to top. Work right front trim in same way, forming 4 buttonholes opposite markers by binding off 3 sts on row 4 for each buttonhole, then casting on 3 sts on the foll row.

collar

With size 9 (5.5 mm) needles and A, cast on 22 (24, 24) sts. K1 row. Cont in St st, casting on 6 sts at beg of next 4 rows, 8 sts at beg of next 2 rows—62 (64, 64) sts. Work in St st for a total of 14 rows. Change to B and k 4 rows. Bind off, then cont down 1 side of collar, pick up and k 8 more sts with B. K4 rows. Bind off. Work other side trim in same way.

finishing

Block pieces to measurements. Sew shoulder seams. Sew side and sleeve seams. Set in sleeves. Sew on collar starting in from the front bands. Sew belt on back so that it overlaps to front, and sew on buttons as shown.

ribbon wrap top

An asymmetrical wrapped top is worked in a loosely knit garter stitch. The neck opening and three-quarter length sleeves are edged with an eyelet stitch for a detailed finish. The top is simply fastened at the side to a comfortable fit. A great addition to any wardrobe—it will look just as stylish over a dress.

SIZE

To fit Small (Medium, Large). Shown in size Medium. This is a standard fitting style with stretchable fit.

FINISHED MEASUREMENTS

- Bust (wrapped) 32½ (34, 35½)" / 82.5 (86, 90) cm
- Long side length 13½ (14, 14½)" / 34 (35.5, 37) cm
- Upper arm 11½ (12¼, 13)" / 29 (31, 33) cm

MATERIALS

 8 (8, 9) x 1¾ oz. (50 g) balls, each approx. 110 yd. (100 m) long, of Lion Brand Yarn *Incredible* (nylon) in #206 Autumn Leaves
- Size 11 (8 mm) needles OR SIZE NECESSARY TO OBTAIN CORRECT GAUGE
- Size 11 (8 mm) circular needle, 24" (60 cm) long
- Size 10½ (6.5 mm) needles for ties only

GAUGE

14 sts and 24 rows = 4" (10 cm) over garter st using size 11 (8 mm) needles. BE SURE TO CHECK THE GAUGE.

NOTE Incs are worked as k1 into front and back of st. Each yo counts as 1 st in the st counts.
Right front and back are knit at same time in 1 piece. Left front is knit separately.

Top

right front

Beg at the right side seam point, with larger needles, cast on 2 sts.
Row 1 (RS) K2.
Row 2 Inc 1 st in each st—4 sts.
Row 3 K4.
Row 4 K1, inc 1 st in each of next 2 sts, k1—6 sts.
Row 5 K6.
Row 6 K2, yo, k2, yo, k2—8 sts.
Row 7 K8.
Row 8 K2, yo, k to last 2 sts, yo, k2—10 sts.
Row 9 K10.
Row 10 Rep row 8—12 sts.
Row 11 K12.
Row 12 K2, k1 into front and back of yo, k to last yo, k1 into front and back of yo, k2—14 sts.
Row 13 (RS) K2, yo, k to last 2 sts, yo, k2—16 sts.
[rep rows 12 and 13] 19 (20, 21) times more, then rep row 12 once—94 (98, 102) sts.

fashion tip Anchor the side tie through the back eyelets to hold the lower edge in place, or in place of the yarn rib tie, use ribbons and draw through all the eyelet openings for contrast trimming.

SEPARATE FOR BACK AND RIGHT FRONT

Next row (RS) K 47 (49, 51) sts and sl to circular needle (or on hold) for right front, k 47 (49, 51) sts for back.

back

Cont on the back sts only, work in garter st inc 1 st each side every 5th row once, then every 6th row 4 times—57 (59, 61) sts. Work even until back side seam (from the separation) measures 6" (15 cm).

SHAPE ARMHOLES

Bind off 3 sts at beg of next 2 rows, then 2 sts at beg of next 2 rows. Dec 1 st each side every other row twice—43 (45, 47) sts. Work even until armhole measures 6½ (7, 7½)" / 16.5 (18, 19) cm.

SHAPE SHOULDERS

Bind off 4 sts at beg of next 6 rows. Bind off rem 19 (21, 23) sts firmly (for back neck).

right front (continued)

Return to the right front 47 (49, 51) sts on hold, and with larger needles k5 rows. Place yarn marker at beg of next (RS) row.

Dec row (RS) K2, yo, sk2p, k to end. Rep dec row every other row 26 (28, 28) times more, AT SAME TIME, work side seam incs (as on back) on the 5th row once, then every 6th row 4 times. When side seam measures 6" (15 cm), shape armhole as on back, binding off 3 sts at armhole once, 2 sts once, dec 1 st every other row twice. When the last yo, sk2p is worked, cont to shape neck with the sk2p only (omit the yo) until there are 12 sts and armhole depth matches the back.

SHAPE SHOULDERS

Bind off 4 sts from armhole edge 3 times.

left front

Separately with larger needles, cast on 47 (49, 51) sts. K2 rows.

Next (eyelet) row (RS) ★ K2tog, yo; rep from ★, ending k1.

Place yarn marker at end of this row. K1 row.

Next row (RS) K to last 5 sts, k3tog, yo, k2. Cont to work as for right front, only with k3tog, yo, k2 at end of RS rows and all other shaping in reverse.

sleeves

Cast on 30 (33, 36) sts. K2 rows.

Next (eyelet) row (RS) ★ K2tog, yo; rep from ★, ending k2 (1, 2). Cont in garter st inc 1 st each side every 8th row 5 times—40 (43, 46) sts. Work even until piece measures 12" (30.5 cm) from beg.

SHAPE CAP

Bind off 3 sts at beg of next 2 rows, then 2 sts at beg of next 2 rows. Dec 1 st each side every other row 4 times, then every 4th row twice. Bind off 2 sts. At beg of next 4 rows, bind off rem 10 (13, 16) sts.

finishing

Do not block pieces. Sew shoulder seams. Leaving a ¾" (2 cm) opening at the lower right side seam (to correspond to the beg of the left lower side edge), sew right side seam. Sew left side seam. Sew sleeve seams. Set in sleeves.

LEFT FRONT TIE

With smaller needles, pick up and k 7 sts along center point from cast-on to yarn markers.

Row 1 (WS) K1, [p1, k1] 3 times. Cont in k1, p1 rib for 23" (58.5 cm). Bind off.

RIGHT FRONT TIE

Work as for left front tie for 8" (20.5 cm).

funky fair isle hat

Bulky alpaca knits up quickly in this cozy hat with earflaps. Trimmed with a crochet border and thick braids, it is sure to keep you warm on the coldest winter days. With the leftover yarns, why not make a second hat? Just remember to alternate the colors to fit the leftover quantities of yarn.

SIZE

To fit one size as shown.

FINISHED MEASUREMENTS

- Head circumference 21" (53 cm)
- Depth 7½" (19 cm)

MATERIALS

- 1 x 1¾ oz. (50 g) ball, approx. 43 yd. (40 m) long, of Tahki Stacy Charles *Alpaka Soft* (alpaca) in #04 White (A), #02 Chocolate (B), #01 Beige (C), and #05 Black (D)
- Set (5) of double-pointed needles (dpn) size 10 (6 mm) OR SIZE NECESSARY TO OBTAIN CORRECT GAUGE
- Size J (6.5 mm) crochet hook
- Stitch markers

GAUGE

12 sts and 15 rnds = 4" (10 cm) over St st using size 10 (6 mm) dpn. BE SURE TO CHECK THE GAUGE.

NOTE Hat is worked in rnds of St st—so k every rnd.

Hat

Beg at lower edge above the earflaps, with A, cast on 64 sts and divide evenly onto 4 needles (16 sts on each needle). Join, being careful not to twist sts, pm to mark beg of rnd. K2 rnds with A.

Rnd 3 [K3 B, k1 A] 16 times.
Rnd 4 Rep rnd 3. Cut color B.
Rnds 5 and 6 Knit with A.
Rnds 7 and 8 Knit with C.
Rnd 9 [K5 C, k1 D, k2 C] 8 times.
Rnd 10 [K4 C, k3 D, k1 C] 8 times.
Rnd 11 [K3 C, k5 D] 8 times.
Rnd 12 [K4 C, k3 D, k1 C] 8 times.
Rnd 13 [K5 C, k1 D, k2 C] 8 times.
Rnds 14 and 15 Knit with C.
Rnds 16 With B, [k6, k2tog] 8 times—56 sts.
Rnds 17 and 18 Knit with B.
Rnd 19 [K3 B, k1 A] 14 times.
Rnd 20 [K1 A, k1 B, k1 A, k1 B] 14 times.
Rnd 21 [K1 A, k1 B, k2tog B, k1 A, k3 B] 7 times—49 sts.
Rnd 22 With B, k2tog, k to end of rnd—48 sts.
Rnd 23 With B, [k4, k2tog] 8 times—40 sts.
Rnd 24 Knit with A.
Rnd 25 With A, [k3, k2tog] 8 times—32 sts.
Rnd 26 [K1 D, k1 A, k2tog A] 8 times—24 sts.
Rnd 27 With A, [k1 k2tog] 8 times—16 sts.
Last rnd With A, [k2tog] 8 times—8 sts.
Cut yarn leaving a long end. Pull through rem sts and draw up tightly to close the top.

earflaps (work 2)

Beg at 8 sts from the center back (with the beg of rnds as the center back), with C pick up and k the next 14 sts.

Row 1 (WS) K2, p10, k2.

Row 2 Knit.

Row 3 K2 C, p4 C, p2 D, p4 C, k2 C.

Row 4 K2 C, sk2p with C, k4 D, k3tog with C, k2 C—10 sts.

Row 5 K2 C, p2 C, k2 D, p2 C, k2 C.

Row 6 With C, k2, sk2p, k3tog, k2.

Row 7 K2, p2, k2.

Bind off. Work 2nd earflap at 8 sts to the opposite side of center back.

crochet trim

With crochet hook and B, join to center back, ch 1, work sc evenly around lower edge of hat, including earflaps. Join and ch 1.

Rnd 2 With A, ★ work 1 sc, ch 1 and skip 1 sc; rep from ★ around, join to first sc. Fasten off A.

Rnd 3 With B, ★ ch 1, work 1 sc in ch 1 space, skip 1 sc; rep from ★ around. Join and fasten off.

finishing

For braids, cut 6 x 34" (86 cm) lengths of all 4 colors. Fold lengths in half and pull one set through each point of earflap and knot at front. Braid together and knot again, leaving a 3" (7.5 cm) fringe.

bobble fringe scarf

A classic but simple cable pattern makes a modern statement knit up as a bright scarf. The crochet bobble fringe adds a fun element to the design, while the bold color is sure to get you noticed. Keep the side edges flat—no blocking needed—by knitting the last few stitches on each row in a slip-stitch rib.

FINISHED MEASUREMENTS

- Length 54" (137 cm)
- Width 11" (28 cm)

MATERIALS

- 3 x 3 oz. (85 g) balls, each approx. 197 yd. (180 m) long, of Lion Brand Yarn *Wool-Ease* (acrylic/wool/rayon) in #112 Red Sprinkles.
- Size 8 (5 mm) needles OR SIZE NECESSARY TO OBTAIN CORRECT GAUGE
- Size 7 (4.5 mm) crochet hook
- Cable needle (cn)

GAUGE

23 sts and 26 rows = 4" (10 cm) across all pat sts using size 8 (5 mm) needles. BE SURE TO CHECK THE GAUGE.

STITCH GLOSSARY

MB Make bobble by [k1, p1, k1, p1, k1] all into 1 st; turn, k5; turn, p1, p3tog, p1; turn, sk2p; turn.

C2R K2tog but leave sts on needle, then k first st again and sl both sts from needles.

3-st RPC Sl 1 st to cn and hold to back, k2, p1 from cn.

3-st LPC Sl 2 sts to cn and hold to front, p1, k2 from cn.

6-st RC Sl 3 sts to cn and hold to back, k3, k3 from cn.

Scarf

Cast on 64 sts.

Row 1 (RS) Sl 2 wyib, p1, k3, p1, k2, p1, k12, p1, k2, p1, k12, p1, k2, p1, k12, p1, k2, p1, k3, p1, sl 2 wyib.

Row 2 P2, k1, p3, k1, p2, k1, p12, k1, p2, k1, p12, k1, p2, k1, p12, k1, p2, k1, p3, k1, p2.

Row 3 Sl 2, p5, k2, p14, k2, p1, [6-st RC] twice, p1, k2, p14, k2, p5, sl 2.

Row 4 Rep row 2.

Row 5 Rep row 1.

Row 6 Rep row 2.

Row 7 Sl 2, p5, k2, p14, k2, p1, k3, 6-st RC, k3, p1, k2, p14, k2, p5, sl 2.

Row 8 Rep row 2.

ZIGZAG PANELS

✱✱ Row 9 (RS) Sl 2, p1, k3, p1, 3-st LPC, p1, [p1, k1] twice, p1, MB, [p1, k1] twice, p2, C2R, p1, k12, p1, C2R, p2, [k1, p1] twice, MB, [p1, k1] twice, p2, 3-st RPC, p1, k3, p1, sl 2.

Row 10 P2, k1, p4, k1, p2, k1, work 11 sts in seed st, k1, p2, k1, p12, k1, p2, k1, work 11 sts in seed st, k1, p2, k1, p4, k1, p2.

Row 11 Sl 2, p6, 3-st LPC, p1, 9 sts in seed st, p2, C2R, p1, [6-st RC] twice, p1, C2R, p2, 9 sts in seed st, p1, 3-st RPC, p6, sl 2.

Row 12 P2, k1, p5, k1, p2, k1, 9 sts in seed st, k2, p2, k1, p12, k1, p2, k2, 9 sts in seed st, k1, p2, k1, p5, k1, p2.

Row 13 Sl 2, p1, k5, p1, 3-st LPC, p1, 8 sts in seed st, p2, C2R, p1, k12, p1, C2R, p2, 8 sts in seed st, p1, 3-st RPC, p1, k5, p1, sl 2.

Row 14 K the knit and p the purl sts only on the outside edges of the zigzag, always purl the sts on the inside edge of the zigzag (next to the center cable), work sts at established in seed st.

Row 15 Sl 2, p8, 3-st LPC, p1, 7 sts in seed st, p2, C2R, p1, k3, 6-st RC, k3, p1, C2R, p2, 7 sts in seed st, p1, 3-st RPC, p8, sl 2.

Row 16 Rep row 14.

Row 17 Sl 2, p1, k7, p1, 3-st LPC, p1, 6 sts in seed st, p2, C2R, p1, k12, p1, C2R,p2, 6 sts in seed st, p1, 3-st RPC, p1, k7, p1, sl 2.

Row 18 Rep row 14.

Row 19 Sl 2, p10, 3-st LPC, p1, 5 sts in seed st, p2, C2R, p1 [6-st RC] twice, p1, C2R, p2, 5 sts in seed st, p1, 3-st RPC, p10, sl 2.

Row 20 Rep row 14.

At this point, the zigzag shifts in the opposite direction.

Row 21 Sl 2, p1, k4, MB, k3, p1, 3-st RPC, p1, 5 sts in seed st, p2, C2R, p1, k12, p1, C2R, p2, 5 sts in seed st, p1, 3-st LPC, p1, k3, MB, k4, p1, sl 2.

Row 22 Rep row 14.

Row 23 Sl 2, p9, 3-st RPC, p1, 6 sts in seed st, p2, C2R, p1, k3, 6-st RC, k3, p1, C2R, p2, 6 sts in seed st, p1, 3-st LPC, p9, sl 2.

Row 24 Rep row 14.

Row 25 Sl 2, p1, k6, p1, 3-st RPC, p1, 7 sts in seed st, p2 C2R, p1, k12, p1, C2R, p2, 7 sts in seed st, p1, 3-st LPC, p1, k6, p1, sl 2.

Row 26 Rep row 14.

Row 27 Sl 2, p7, 3-st RPC, p1, 8 sts in seed st, p2, C2R, p1, [6-st RC] twice, p1, C2R, p2, 8 sts in seed st, p1, 3-st LPC, p7, sl 2.

Row 28 Rep row 14.

Row 29 Sl 2, p1, k4, p1, 3-st RPC, p1, 9 sts in seed st, p2, C2R, p1, k12, p1, C2R, p2, 9 sts in seed st, p1, 3-st LPC, p1, k4, p1, sl 2.

Row 30 Rep row 14.

Row 31 Sl 2, p5, 3-st RPC, p1, 10 sts in seed st, p2, C2R, p1, k3, 6-st RC, k3, p1, C2R, p2, 10 sts in seed st, p1, 3-st LPC, p5, sl 2.

Row 32 Rep row 14 ★★.

Rep between ★★s (24 rows) for pat st a total of 13 times more. Then work rows 1–8 once. Bind off.

finishing

Do not block.

BOBBLE TRIM

With crochet hook, join yarn to one lower corner of bottom edge with a Sl st, ★ ch 4, [yo and draw up a loop in 2nd ch from hook] 5 times for bobble, yo and draw through all loops on hook, ch 4, skip 4 sts at edge, Sl st in next st; rep from ★ across edge 10 times more. Fasten off. Repeat for other bottom edge.

ribbed cocoon shrug

A simple rectangle is worked in an easy rib and lace stitch then seamed to form the shrug style as shown. This is a perfect beginner project that's very easy to knit, super easy to finish, and a lot of fun to wear. A must-have fashion item that will be individual to you—and the envy of your friends.

SIZE

To fit Small (Medium, Large). Shown in size Medium. This is a standard-fitting style.

FINISHED MEASUREMENTS

- Rectangle width 31 (32, 33)" / 78.5 (81, 84) cm
- Rectangle length 23½" (59.5 cm)

MATERIALS

 8 (8, 9) x 1¾ oz. (50 g) hanks, each approx. 108 yd. (99 m) long, of Classic Elite Yarns *Miracle* (alpaca/tencel) in #3334 Martin's Purple
- Size 6 (4 mm) circular needle, 24" (60 cm) long, OR SIZE NECESSARY TO OBTAIN CORRECT GAUGE
- Size F/5 (4 mm) crochet hook

GAUGE

24 sts and 32 rows = 4" (10 cm) over perforated rib pat using size 6 (4 mm) needles. BE SURE TO CHECK THE GAUGE.

PERFORATED RIB PATTERN

Over a multiple of 6 sts plus 1.
Row 1 (WS) P1, ★ k1, yo to M1, p3tog, yo to M1, k1, p1; rep from ★ to end.
Row 2 (RS) ★ K1, p1, k3, p1; rep from ★, ending k1.
Row 3 P1, ★ k1, p3, k1, p1; rep from ★ to end.
Row 4 Rep row 2.
Rep rows 1–4 for perforated rib pat.

Shrug

Cast on 187 (193, 199) sts. Work in perforated rib pat for (189 rows) or 23½" (59.5 cm). Bind off. Leave yarn attached.

finishing

Do not block. With crochet hook, ch 48 with the working yarn. Sl st in 2nd ch from hook and in each ch to end. Join and secure. Fasten off. Work a ch 48 tie on opposite edge in same way. Place yarn marker at 4½" (11.5 cm) from each top (bound-off) edge and 4½" (11.5 cm) from lower (cast-on) edge. Seam the rectangle tog along these 4½" (11.5 cm) edges. Tie at front as shown in the photo.

fashion tip Use a narrow ribbon in place of the crocheted ties and pull through the openwork pattern at center front.

laced suede skirt

This pull-on skirt with flared insets at the hem is edged with cross-stitch embroidery.
The long tie belt is created by twisting yarn together to make a cord. The cord is
decorated with beads and tassels—craft stores have got a great variety of beads at
the moment, so let them inspire your embellishment.

SIZE
To fit Small (Medium, Large). Shown in size Small.
This is a standard fitting style.

FINISHED MEASUREMENTS
- Hip 36 (38, 40)" / 91.5 (96.5, 101.5) cm
- Waist 26 (28, 30)" / 66 (71, 76) cm
- Length 29" (73.5 cm)

MATERIALS
- **3** 11 (12, 13) x 1¾ oz. (50 g) balls, each approx. 120 yd. (111 m) long, of Berroco *Suede* (nylon) in #3717 Wild Bill Hickcock (A)
- 1 x 1¾ oz. (50 g) ball approx. 120 yd. (111 m) long, of Berroco *Suede* (nylon) in #3737 Roy Rogers (B)
- Size 7 (4.5 mm) and 8 (5 mm) needles OR SIZE NECESSARY TO OBTAIN CORRECT GAUGE
- Size 7 (4.5 mm) crochet hook
- Tapestry needle (for embroidery)
- 2 x ⅜" (1 cm) round wood beads, and 4 x ¼" (5 mm) decorative brass beads.
- 1 yd. (90 cm) of ¾" (2 cm) wide elastic.

GAUGE
19 sts and 28 rows = 4" (10 cm) over St st using larger
needles. BE SURE TO CHECK THE GAUGE.

Skirt

back

With larger needles and A, cast on 213 (218, 223) sts.

Row 1 (RS) K36 (38, 40), [p2, k47, p2] for first flare, k39(40,41), [p2, k47, p2] for 2nd flare, k36 (38, 40).

Row 2 P36 (38, 40), [k2, p47, k2], p39 (40, 41), [k2, p47, k2], p36 (38, 40).

Flare dec row (RS) K to first flare, ★ p2, skp, k to last 2 sts in flare, k2tog, p2 ★, k to 2nd flare, rep between ★s once, k to end.

Next row Work even in pat as established.

Rep the last 2 rows 21 times more. There are 3 k sts between the p2 ridges in each flare.

Next dec row (RS) K to first flare, ★ p2, sk2p, p2 ★, k to 2nd flare, rep between ★s once, k to end.

Next row (WS) P to the 5-st section in the flare, ★ k1, sk2p k1 ★, p to the 2nd 5-st section in the flare, rep between ★s once, p to end.

Next row (RS) K to the first flare, p2tog, p1, k to the 2nd flare, p2tog, p1, k to end—115 (120, 125) sts.

All sts are in St st with 2 purl-2 sections that will cont above each flare to end of piece. Cont in pats as established for 5 rows more.

Side dec row (RS) K1, skp, work to last 3 sts, k2tog, k1. Rep side dec row every 6th row 4 times more, every 8th row 5 times, every 10th row 5 times—85 (90, 95) sts. Work 1 row even.

Next row (RS) Work side dec row.

Rep side dec row every 4th row twice, every other row 8 times—63 (68, 73) sts. Bind off.

front

Work same as back.

finishing

For front waistband, picking up and k sts through the back loop only, pick up 63 (68, 73) sts with smaller needles and A. K1 row, p2 rows, k2 rows, p1 row. Then beg with a p row, work 5 rows in St st (for waistband hem). Bind off. Cut elastic to fit waist plus 1" (2.5 cm) for seaming. Seam into a circle. From WS, Sl st the side seams tog using crochet hook and working through one st at each edge. With B, work cross-st embroidery (see below) over the p-2 sections going into 1 loop at k st each side of these sections. Work waistband cross-st embroidery in same way. Fold waistband over elastic and baste in to place.

TIE BELT

Make a 43" (109 cm) length twisted cord belt (see page 104). Add 3 beads to each end of belt and tie an overhand knot to hold in place. Cut several 13" (33 cm) lengths of yarn and thread through the knot to make a tassel on each end. Wrap one of the strands around each tassel and knot to secure. Block the lower edge lightly, if necessary.

finishing tip If desired, add a ch-8 loop at each waistband seam to hold the cord belt in place.

cross stitch Bring the needle up at the bottom left-hand corner and take it down at the top right-hand corner. Cross this stitch from the bottom right to the top left.

feather-weight scarf

Garter stitch worked in baby-weight yarn is alternated with stockinette stitch in cotton thread for a sheer stripe effect in this summer scarf. An excellent project for a beginner—very fast and easy to knit.

FINISHED MEASUREMENTS

- Length 60" (152 cm)
- Width 4½" (11.5 cm)

MATERIALS

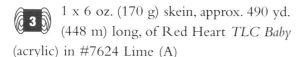

- 1 x 6 oz. (170 g) skein, approx. 490 yd. (448 m) long, of Red Heart *TLC Baby* (acrylic) in #7624 Lime (A)
- 1 x 400 yd. (366 m) long ball of Coats & Clark *Aunt Lydia's Fine Crochet Thread*, size 20, in #0201 White (B)
- Size 7 (4 mm) circular needle, 24" (60 cm) long OR SIZE NECESSARY TO OBTAIN CORRECT GAUGE

GAUGE

16 sts = 4" (10 cm); 7 color stripes = 4½" (11.5 cm) wide over garter and St st stripe pat using size 7 (4 mm) needles. BE SURE TO CHECK THE GAUGE.

NOTE Stripe pattern is formed by working 4 knit rows (garter st) with lime (A) and 3 St st rows with White (B). A long length of yarn is joined on every row then cut, and knotted at both ends to form the feathery self fringe.

Scarf

Beg at the long edge with A, cast on 240 sts. Cut yarn leaving a 10 to 12" (25 to 30 cm) long end.
Row 1 (RS) Leaving long end, join A and knit. Cut yarn, turn.
Row 2 Leaving long end, join A and knit. Cut yarn, turn.
Rows 3 and 4 Rep last 2 rows once more.
Row 5 (RS) Leaving long end, join B and knit. Cut yarn, turn.
Row 6 (WS) Leaving long end, join B and purl. Cut yarn, turn.
Row 7 Rep row 5, do not turn at end.
Beg on the RS for next stripe row, work rows 1–7 for stripe pat 5 times more. Work rows 1–4 once more. There are 7 x A stripes. Bind off.

finishing

Double knot each fringe. Trim ends to create a 1" (2.5 cm) fringe. Block to measurements to lay flat.

> **finishing tip** To ensure that the ends do not unravel while working, knot on every row as you complete it.

classic fair isle shrug

Fair Isle strips run across a moss green background in this easy shrug style with wraparound fronts and set-in sleeves. The body is knit in one piece on circular needles, and the sleeves are picked up around the armholes and worked from the top down. A classic garment to have in your wardrobe for slightly cooler days.

SIZE

To fit one size, as shown.

FINISHED MEASUREMENTS

- Total length of wraparound piece 40" (101.5 cm)
- Body length at back 10½" (26.5 cm)
- Upper arm 14" (35.5 cm)

MATERIALS

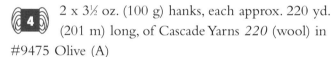

- 2 x 3½ oz. (100 g) hanks, each approx. 220 yd. (201 m) long, of Cascade Yarns *220* (wool) in #9475 Olive (A)
- 1 x 3½ oz. (100 g) hank approx. 220 yd. (201 m) long, of Cascade Yarns *220* (wool) in #9476 Maize (B), #9341 Wine (C), #9441 Heather Rose (D), #7612 Bronze Tweed (E), #2415 Sunflower (F), and #7618 Charcoal Tweed (G)
- Size 7 (4.5 mm) and 8 (5 mm) circular needles in both 16" (40 cm) and 24" (60 cm) lengths OR SIZE NECESSARY TO OBTAIN CORRECT GAUGE

GAUGE

19 sts and 22 rows = 4" (10 cm) over St st using larger needles. BE SURE TO CHECK THE GAUGE.

FAIR ISLE PATTERN BANDS

PATTERN BAND 1

Worked in Wine (C), Bronze Tweed (E), and Sunflower (F) over a multiple of 4 sts plus 2 and 3 rows.

Row 1 (RS) ★ K2 C, k2 E; rep from ★, ending k2 C.

Row 2 P1 E, p1 F, ★ p1 F, p2 E, p1 F; rep from ★ to end.

Row 3 Rep row 1.

These 3 rows complete Pat Band 1.

PATTERN BAND 2

Worked in Maize (B), Heather Rose (D), Olive (A), and Wine (C). Over a multiple of 6 sts plus 4 and 5 rows.

Row 1 (RS) With B, knit.

Row 2 ★ P1 B, p1 A, p2 B, p1 D, p1 B; rep from ★, ending p1 B, p1 A, p2 B.

Row 3 K2 B, k1 A, k1 B, ★ k1 D, k1 C, k1 D, k1 B, k1 A, k1 B; rep from ★ to end.

Row 4 Rep row 2.

Row 5 With B, knit.

These 5 rows complete Pat Band 2.

PATTERN BAND 3

Worked in Heather Rose (D), Charcoal Tweed (G), and Sunflower (F).

Over a multiple of 8 sts plus 6 and 6 rows.

Row 1 (RS) ★ K2 G, k1 D, k2 G, k3 D; rep from ★, ending k2 G, k1 D, k2 G, k1 D.

Row 2 P2 G, p3 D, p1 G, ★ p1 G, p1 D, p2 G, p3 D, p1 G; rep from ★ to end.

Row 3 ★ K2 F, k1 G, k2 F, k3 G; rep from ★, ending k2 F, k1 G, k2 F, k1 G.

Row 4 P2 F, p3 G, p1 F, ★ p1 F, p1 G, p2 F, p3 G, p1 F; rep from ★ to end.

Row 5 Rep row 1.

Row 6 Rep row 2.
These 6 rows complete Pat Band 3.

NOTE Shrug is made in one piece beg at the lower edge that wraps around to form the fronts. The "sides" or row edges of this lower edge piece form the front shoulders. The sleeves are picked up around the armholes and worked down to the cuff edges.

Shrug

With smaller size (longer) circular needles and G, cast on 190 sts. Work in k1, p1 rib for 4 rows.
Row 5 (RS) With F, knit.
Row 6 With F, work in established k1, p1 rib. Change to larger size (longer) circular needle. With A, work in St st for 4 rows. Work Pat Band 1 for 3 rows. With A, work in St st for 3 rows. Work Pat Band 2 for 5 rows. With A, work in St st for 3 rows. Work in Pat Band 1 for 3 rows. With A, p1 row.
Next row (RS) With A, bind off 50 sts (right front armhole), k until there are 90 sts on needle, with a 2nd ball of yarn, bind off rem 50 sts (left front armhole). The beg and end pieces will finish later by wrapping around the front armholes and the sides of the rows are the front shoulders.

back

Cont with A only to end of back, bind off 5 sts at beg of next 2 rows, 3 sts at beg of next 4 rows, 2 sts at beg of next 2 rows, 1 st at beg of next 2 rows—62 sts. Work even until back measures 4½" (11.5 cm) from the initial 50-st bind off.

SHAPE SHOULDERS
Bind off 4 sts at beg of next 6 rows, 5 sts at beg of next 2 rows—28 sts.

BACK NECK BAND
Change to smaller size (shorter) needles and k1 (RS) row with F. Work 1 row in k1, p1 rib with F. K1 row with G. Work 3 rows in k1, p1 rib with G. Bind off in rib. Block lightly. Sew shoulder seams by matching sides of shrug to the back shaped shoulders and the back neckband to the lower rib.

sleeves

Using larger size (shorter) needle and A, beg at the inside center of the armhole, pick up and k 50 sts from front armhole and 28 sts from back—78 sts. Working back and forth in rows on the circular needle, work in St st and color bands as foll: dec 1 st each side every 6th row 8 times, every 4th row 7 times in this color sequence: ★ 3 rows A, 6 rows Pat Band 3, 3 rows A, 3 rows Pat Band 1, 3 rows A, 5 rows Pat Band 2, 3 rows A, 3 rows Pat Band 1; rep from ★ once more, then work 3 rows A, 6 rows Pat Band 3, 3 rows A, 3 rows Pat Band 1, 4 rows A. At this point there are 48 sts. Sleeve measures approx. 15½" (39.5 cm) from the pick-up line. Change to smaller size (shorter) circular needle. K1 row with F. Work 1 row in k1, p1 rib with F. K1 row with G. Work 3 rows in k1, p1 rib with G. Bind off. Block sleeves lightly and sew sleeve seams.

knitting tip For easier working, chart color band repeats in color on graph paper before beg to knit. Tape a short length of each yarn to the edge of the chart as a key to remind yourself which yarn you are referring to each time.

square neck peasant top

Easy-to-knit straight falling pieces are gathered to fit the open lace-work strips that are sewn in place. The top can also be adjusted for a more perfect fit using the drawstring threaded through the lace openings. This is the perfect top to dress up or down, according to the demands of your day.

SIZE

To fit one size, Small/Medium. This size is adjustable at the bustline, where a shorter or longer piece of lace can be cut to desired fit and then the knit fabric gathered to fit this measurement.

FINISHED MEASUREMENTS

- Bust 38" (96.5 cm)
- Length 23" (58.5 cm)
- Upper arm 15" (38 cm)

MATERIALS

2 7 x 2½ oz. (70 g) balls, each approx. 168 yd. (154 m) long, of Lion Brand Yarns *Microspun* (microfiber acrylic) in #100 Lily White
- Size 4 (3.5 mm) needles OR SIZE NECCESSARY TO OBTAIN THE CORRECT GAUGE
- Size E/4 (3.5 mm) crochet hook
- 3 yd. (2.7 m) of Mokuba cotton lace #61093 (narrow) and #61091 (wide) in #00 White
- Matching white thread
- Sewing needle

GAUGE

24 sts and 32 rows = 4" (10 cm) over St st using size 4 (3.5 mm) needles. BE SURE TO CHECK THE GAUGE.

Top

back and front (make 2)

NOTE The front and the back are the same. Cast on 138 sts. K 6 rows (for garter st). Cont in St st until piece measures 15" (38 cm) from beg.
Next row (RS) [K4, k2tog] 23 times—115 sts. Bind off.

sleeves

UPPER SLEEVE (MAKE 2)

Cast on 60 sts. K 1 row.
Row 2 (WS) [P4, inc 1 st in next st] 12 times—72 sts. Cont in St st inc 1 st each side every 6th row 6 times—72 sts. Work even until piece measures 6½" (16.5 cm) from beg.

SHAPE CAP

Bind off 3 sts at beg of next 20 rows. Bind off rem 12 sts.

LOWER SLEEVE (MAKE 2)

Cast on 72 sts. K6 rows (for garter st). Cont in St st for 6" (15 cm), ending with a RS row.
Next row (WS) [P4, p2tog] 12 times—60 sts. Bind off.

finishing

Block pieces lightly. Sew the side seams. Gather the front and back of the top to measure 38" (96.5 cm) using a strand of yarn to baste the gathers. Carefully sew the wide lace across the gathered top. Gather the upper sleeve at the lower edge to measure 13" (33 cm) and sew narrow lace across this gathered piece. Gather and sew the lower sleeve to opposite side of lace in same way. Gather the cap of the sleeve to fit a measurement of 13" (33 cm) and sew the narrow lace across the cap. Measuring from cap of sleeve place a thread marker 3" (7.5 cm) down each side of sleeves. Sew underarm seams together, leaving top 3" (7.5 cm) free, and leaving a 1" (2.5 cm) opening (for slit) at lower sleeve edge.

JOIN SLEEVE TO BODY

Matching underarm and side seams, pin the 3" (7.5 cm) on either side of underarm (sleeve) seam to body of sweater attaching along the front and back pieces under the wide lace edging. Sew in place.

CROCHETED TIE

With crochet hook, ch for 52" (132 cm) to make tie to draw through the bustline lace. Thread through openings in lace and tie in front.

baby doll top

A sideways-knit bodice in two by two rib provides a body contouring fit for this baby doll tank top with a simple openwork lace skirt. Worked in denim style yarn for an easy going casual look, it could be knit in a variety of different colors for different effects—baby doll pink is the classic color for this piece.

SIZE

To fit Small (Medium, Large). Shown in size Small. This is a close fitting style.

FINISHED MEASUREMENTS

- Bust 32 (34, 36)" / 81 (86, 91.5) cm
- Length from top of shoulder 26½" (67 cm)

MATERIALS

4 3 x 3½ oz. (100 g) balls, each approx. 196 yd. (179 m) long, of Bernat *Denim Style* (acrylic/cotton) in #426 Weathered Rose
- Size 6 (4 mm) and 8 (5 mm) needles OR SIZE NECESSARY TO OBTAIN CORRECT GAUGE
- Size 7 (4.5 mm) crochet hook

GAUGE

16 sts and 24 rows = 4" (10 cm) over k2, p2 rib (slightly stretched) using size 6 (4 mm) needles. BE SURE TO CHECK THE GAUGE.

OBLIQUE PATTERN STITCH

Over an even number of sts.
Row 1 (RS) K1, ★ yo to M1, k2tog, rep from ★, ending k1.
Rows 2 and 4 Purl.
Row 3 K2, ★ yo to M1, k2tog, rep from ★ to end.
Rep rows 1-4 for oblique pat st.

Top

back bodice

Beg at the side seam, with smaller needles, cast on 31 sts.

Row 1 (RS) ★ K2, p2; rep from ★, ending k2, p1.

Row 2 K the knit and p the purl sts.

Dec row 3 K2, p2tog, rib to end.

Rep dec row every 2nd row 7 times more—23 sts. Work even until piece measures 11 (12, 13)" / 28 (30.5, 33) cm from beg.

Inc row (RS) K2, M1 st, rib to end. Rep inc row (working incs into k2, p2 rib) every 2nd row 7 times more—31 sts. Work 1 row even.

Bind off in rib.

front bodice

NOTE Front side seam is shaped and will fit to the back straight seam. Read before beg to knit.

Beg at top edge of bodice, with smaller needles, cast on 6 sts.

Row 1 (RS) K2, place marker, p2, k2.

Next row (WS) Cast on 5 sts, turn and k1, p2, k2, p2, k2, p2. Cont to cast on 5 sts at beg of the next 4 WS rows, AT SAME TIME, shape top of bodice beg on next RS row by M1 in rib at the marker and rep the M1 inc every row 15 times more—47 sts. Place a yarn marker at top (shaped) edge on last row. Work even until piece measures 11 (12, 13)" / 28 (30.5, 33) cm from the yarn marker.

Next row (RS) K1, skp, rib to end.

Next row (WS) Rib to last 3 sts, p2tog tbl, p1. [Rep the last 2 rows] 7 times more, AT SAME TIME, when the lower edge measures 14 (15, 16)" / 35.5 (38, 40.5) cm, bind off 5 sts from this edge every WS row 5 times, 6 sts once.

skirt

Working along the back bodice with size 8 (5 mm) needles, pick up and k 46 (48, 51) sts along the lower edge.

Row 1 (WS) [P1 into front and back of next st] 46 (48, 51) times—92 (96, 102) sts.

Beg with row 1, work in oblique pat st for 16" (40.5 cm) from pick up, ending with row 2 or 4. K2 rows. Bind off knitwise. Work front bodice in same way. Sew side seams.

straps

With crochet hook, join yarn at top of bodice point on one front side, ch 36, join the chain to top of back bodice at the inside straight edge, turn Sl st in each ch and secure at chain front. Work 2nd strap in same way.

> **finishing tip** The skirt can be worked in rounds on a circular needle for a quick finish. Just work the 2nd and 4th rnds as knit, instead of purl.

garter stitch capelet

A simple garter stitch and streamline shaping make this a perfect beginner project. The reverse stockinette stitch edging is simple but effective, and the large vintage button adds glamour in an instant. Add your own individual touch to the piece by changing the color, or choosing a different fastening.

SIZE

To fit one size, as shown. This is a standard fitting style.

FINISHED MEASUREMENTS

- Lower edge 51" (129.5 cm)
- Depth 12" (30.5 cm)

MATERIALS

- 4 x 1¾ oz. (50 g) balls, each approx. 150 yd. (137 m) long, of Classic Elite *Princess* (merino/viscose/cashmere/angora/nylon) in #3460 Greatest Green
- Size 7 (4.5 mm) circular needle, 24" (60 cm) long, OR SIZE NECESSARY TO OBTAIN CORRECT GAUGE
- Decorative button 1½" x 1¼" (4 cm x 3 cm)
- Stitch markers

GAUGE

19 sts and 32 rows = 4" (10 cm) over garter st using size 7 (4.5 mm) needles. BE SURE TO CHECK THE GAUGE.

Capelet

Beg at lower edge, cast on 242 sts.
Row 1 (RS) K59, place marker, k124, place marker, k59. Cont in garter st (k every row) for 7 rows more.
Dec row (RS) ★ K to 3 sts before marker, k2tog, k1, sl marker, k1, k2tog; rep from ★ once more, k to end—238 sts. Rep dec row every 8th row once more, then every 6th row 4 times, then every 4th row 5 times—198 sts. Work 1 row even.

SHAPE SHOULDERS

Next row (RS) Rep dec row. Cont to work dec row every 2nd row 9 times more—158 sts. There are 38 sts before first marker, 82 sts in back and 38 sts after 2nd marker. Work 1 row even.

SHAPE FRONT NECK

NOTE Shoulder shaping and neck shaping are worked simultaneously. Read before cont to knit.
Next row (RS) Sl first 4 sts to a holder, rejoin and rep dec row at markers, k to last 4 sts and sl these sts to a holder, turn.
Bind off 2 sts at beg of next 2 rows, 1 st at beg of next 20 rows, AT SAME TIME, cont to work shoulder dec row at markers every RS row 7 times more, then work dec row 2 on next RS row as foll:
Dec row 2 (RS) ★ K to 4 sts before marker, k3tog, k1, sl marker, k1, k3tog; rep from ★ once, k to end. [Rep dec row 2] 3 times more. Bind off rem 62 sts.

Row 3 Knit.
Row 4 Purl. Bind off knitwise.

NECK EDGE

Pick up and k 31 sts from right front neck edge, 51 sts from back neck, 31 sts from left front neck edge—113 sts. Work 4-row rolled edge as before. Sew on button opposite buttonhole 1" (2.5 cm) from the edge.

finishing

LEFT FRONT ROLLED EDGE

With size 7 (4.5 mm) circular needle, pick up and k 41 along center left front edge (1 st for every garter ridge).
Row 1 (WS) Purl.
Row 2 Purl.
Row 3 Knit.
Row 4 Purl. Bind off knitwise.

RIGHT FRONT ROLLED EDGE

Pick up sts as for left front edge.
Row 1 (WS) P2, bind off 4 sts (for buttonhole), purl to end.
Row 2 Purl, casting on 4 sts over the bound-off sts of previous row.

finishing tip To easily pick up sts for the edges, use a crochet hook and go into the indent space between the garter ridges. Working this way gives a "selvage seam" at the back of the work and produces a more stable edge.

trio tweed jacket

Two colors of suede yarn form the stripe details on this easy-fit jacket worked in a surface-texture metallic tweed yarn and finished with slit cuffs, and a stylish ribbon tie. The edges are trimmed with a simple garter stitch finish.

SIZE

To fit Small (Medium, Large). Shown in size Medium. This is a standard fitting style.

FINISHED MEASUREMENTS

- Bust (closed) 35 (37, 39)" / 89 (94, 99) cm
- Length 21½ (22, 22½)" / 54.5 (56, 57) cm
- Upper arm 12½ (13½, 14½)" / 32 (34, 37) cm

MATERIALS

- **5** 9 (9, 10) x 1¾ oz. (50 g) balls, each approx. 55 yd. (50 m) long, of Berroco *Lavish* (nylon/wool/polyester/acrylic) in #7320 Shanelle (A)
- 3 x 1¾ oz. (50 g) balls, each approx. 120 yd. (111 m) long, of Berroco *Suede* (nylon) in #3719 Texas Rose (B) and #3716 Maverick (C)
- Size 9 (5.5 mm) needles OR SIZE NECESSARY TO OBTAIN CORRECT GAUGE
- Size 10 (6 mm) needles for casting on
- Size 7 (4.5 mm) crochet hook for sl stitching pieces together
- 1 yd. (90 cm) of 6 mm wide Mokuba silk velvet ribbon #2600, in #9 Mauve

GAUGE

16 sts and 19 rows = 4" (10 cm) over double knit check pat using size 9 (5.5 mm) needles. BE SURE TO CHECK THE GAUGE.

DOUBLE KNIT CHECK PATTERN

Over an even number of sts.
A = Shanelle *Lavish*, B = Texas Rose *Suede*,
C = Maverick *Suede*
Cast on with A.
Rows 1 and 2 With A, knit.
Row 3 With B, k1, ★ k into eye of st below next st on needle (k1-b), k1; rep from ★, ending k1.
Row 4 With B, knit.
Row 5 With A, k1, ★ k1, k1-b; rep from ★, ending k1.
Row 6 With A, knit.
Row 7 With C, rep row 3.
Row 8 With C, rep row 4.
Row 9 Rep row 5.
Row 10 Rep row 6.
Rep rows 3–10 (8-row rep) for double knit check pat.

NOTE For easier working, work all incs and decs on WS (k) rows.

fashion tip For a standard length sleeve, add 4" (10 cm) to the finished length and have more rows between the increases for the best slant.

Jacket

back

With larger needles and A, cast on 74 (78, 82) sts.
Change to size 9 (5.5 mm) needles and work in
double knit check pat for 7 rows.
Dec row (WS) K1, k2tog, k to last 3 sts, k2tog, k1.
Rep dec row every 6th row twice more, every 4th
row 3 times—62 (66, 70) sts. Work even until piece
measures 9" (23 cm) from beg.
Inc row (WS) K1, inc 1 st in next st, k to last 2 sts,
inc 1 st in next st, k1.
Rep inc row every 4th row 3 times more—70
(74, 78) sts.
Work even until piece measures 13" (33 cm)
from beg.

SHAPE ARMHOLES

Bind off 3 sts at beg of next 2 rows, 2 sts at beg
of next 4 rows. Dec 1 st each side every other row
2 (3, 4) times—52 (54, 56) sts. Work even until
armhole measures 7 (7½, 8)" / 18 (19, 20.5) cm.

NECK AND SHOULDER SHAPING

Bind off 3 sts at beg of next 4 (2, 0) rows, 4 sts at
beg of next 4 (6, 8) rows, AT SAME TIME as the
3rd shoulder bind-off, bind off center 16 sts and
working both sides at once, bind off 4 sts from each
neck edge once.

left front

With larger needles and A, cast on 38 (40, 42) sts.
Change to size 9 (5.5 mm) needles and work in
double knit check pat for 7 rows. Dec 1 st at end
of next WS row (side seam edge), then rep dec
every 6th row twice more, every 4th row 3 times—
32 (34, 36) sts. Work even until piece measures
9" (23 cm) from beg. Inc 1 st at end of next WS
row (side seam edge) then rep inc every 4th row
3 times more—36 (38, 40) sts. Work even until
piece measures 13" (33 cm) from beg.

ARMHOLE SHAPING

From armhole edge, bind off 3 sts once, 2 sts
twice, dec 1 st every other row 2 (3, 4) times—

27 (28, 29) sts. Work even until piece measures 17 (17½, 18)" / 43 (44.5, 45.5) cm from beg, then work neck shaping as foll:

NECK SHAPING

Next row (WS) Bind off 4 sts (neck edge), work to end. Cont to shape neck, binding off 3 sts once more, 2 sts 3 times—14 (15, 16) sts rem after all armhole incs are completed. When same length as back, shape shoulder as on back.

right front

Work as for left front, reversing shaping.

sleeves

With larger needles and A, cast on 40 sts. Change to size 9 (5.5 mm) needles and work in double knit check pat, inc 1 st each side every 8th row 7 times—50 (54, 58) sts. Work even until piece measures 13½" (34 cm) from beg.

SHAPE CAP

Bind off 3 sts at beg of next 2 rows, 2 sts at beg of next 2 rows. Dec 1 st each side every 2nd row 8 (10, 12) times. Bind off 2 sts at beg of next 4 rows. Bind off rem 16 sts.

finishing

Block pieces to measurements. With size 9 (5.5 mm) needles and C, pick up and k 1 st in every cast-on st along lower back. K2 rows. Bind off. Rep this 2-row edge for fronts. For sleeve slits, pick up and k 9 sts along 2½" (6.5 cm) of the slit and work in same way. For sleeve cuffs, pick up and k 43 sts and work in same way. Using crochet hook and C, Sl st shoulders tog, side and sleeve seams up to the slits, and set in sleeves. Work the 2-row edge along the center fronts picking up and k 48 (50, 53) sts, then 67 sts around the neck edge. Draw the ribbon through the sts at empire-waist height, as shown. Knot ends of ribbon to hold in place.

how to get started

This section includes all the basic techniques you will need to get started, from casting on for the first time, to shaping, and binding off your work. If you are new to knitting, read through all the techniques carefully, and practice any tricky bits until you are confident enough to try one of the easier patterns.

Maintaining gauge

holding the needles

The position of the needles is crucial to the finished gauge of your knitting. Some knitters hold both needles evenly in front of them, while others secure one needle under the right arm and let the left needle drop diagonally. Yet another style is to secure both needles, one under each arm. It does not matter which style you choose, as long as you feel comfortable, without any strain on your hands, back, or neck, and can work easily.

Hold the needles evenly in front of the body, with the hands taking equal weight. This method is favored by beginners knitting for the first time.

Here the right-hand needle is held firmly under the arm, leaving the right hand free to tension the yarn. The weight of the knitting is held under your arm.

holding the yarn

Holding the yarn will come with practice and may feel awkward at the start. Everyone finds a way to tension the yarn so that it flows evenly through the fingers. These instructions are for a right-handed knitter.

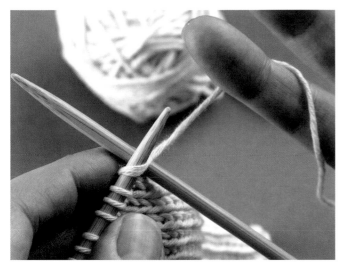

1 Hold the needles in your left hand. With your right palm upper-most, take the yarn round your little finger.

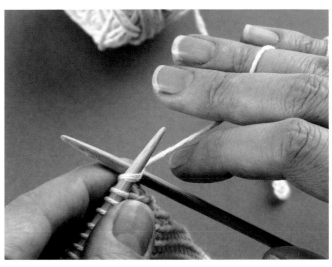

2 As you turn your right hand over, wrap the yarn over your ring finger and under your middle finger.

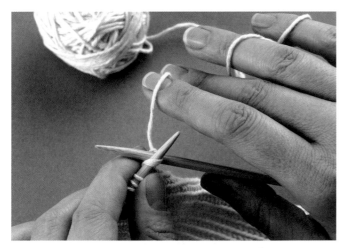

3 Your index finger will control the yarn; hold your hand so that this finger can easily loop over the needles. To maintain tension, readjust this movement from time to time.

reading the label All knitting yarns will have a number or date on the ball band, or inside the cone, that relates to the batch in which it was dyed. It is essential to check this number when purchasing yarn, making sure that all your balls are from the same batch. Although it may not be obvious at this stage, any yarn from a different dye vat will definitely stand out when the garment is finished.

Making a slipknot
This is the essential first step in knitting. Making a slipknot will allow you to begin casting on for a new project.

1 Make a loop by passing the right side of the yarn over the left.

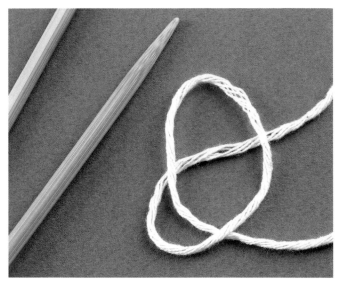

2 Pass the tail end under the loop. Now pass it through the first loop.

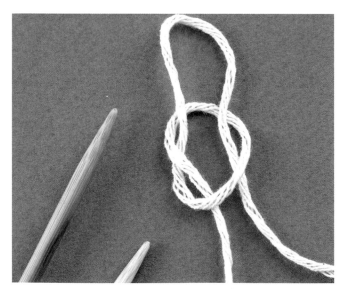

3 Pull the tail end to secure the slipknot.

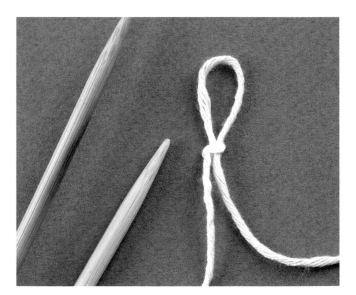

4 Adjust the loop to the correct size for your thumb or knitting needle, depending on which cast-on method you use.

Casting on
This is the first row of your knitting and usually creates the bottom edge of your work. Find a way that works for you and your project.

long end casting on
This is also known as the "thumb" method. To calculate the amount of yarn needed for the long end, estimate the finished length of the cast-on edge, and multiply by three.

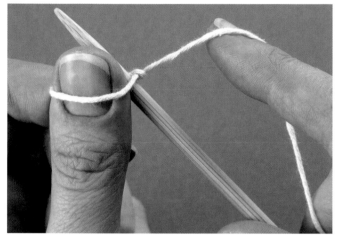

1 Make a slipknot with your yarn, leaving a tail that is long enough to cast on the number of stitches required. Place the loop on your thumb, and insert the point from the right needle into the loop.

2 With your right hand, wrap the yarn around the point of the needle and between the needle and your thumb.

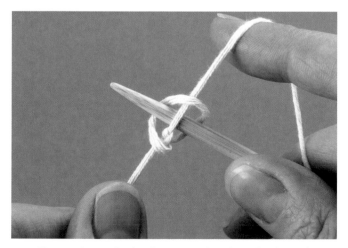

3 Draw through the loop on the thumb, then slip the loop over the edge of the needle, knit the loop and make a stitch.

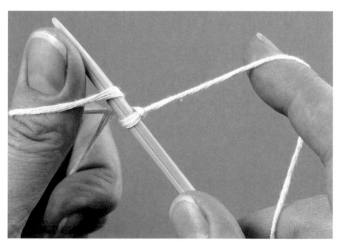

4 Keep going until you have the required number of stitches on the needle.

casting on with two needles

This method works only if the first row of knitting will be worked into the back of the stitches in the casting-on row. If you do not do this, the edge of your work will be loopy.

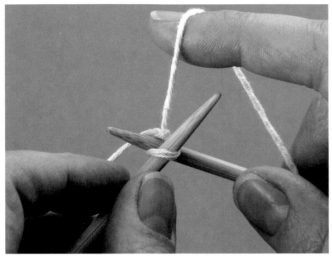

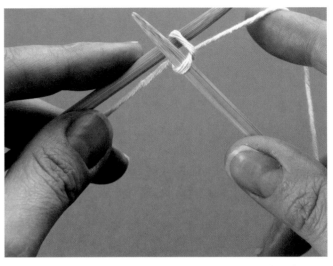

1 Make a slip knot and put it onto the left needle. Put the right needle into the loop so that it passes under the left.

2 Pass the yarn between the needles and take the yarn through the first loop with the right needle.

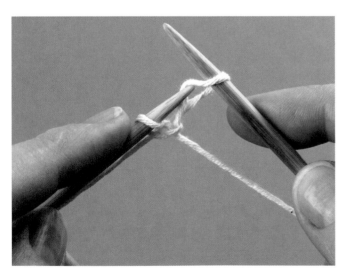

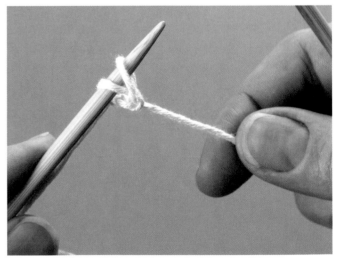

3 Then pass the second loop from the right needle to the left.

4 Repeat by putting the right needle into the last stitch on the left needle until you have made the required number of stitches.

cable casting on

This method makes a strong edge and is more decorative than the other casting-on methods, though it may not be as elastic. Follow the method for casting on with two needles for the first two stitches, then make the remaining stitches as follows.

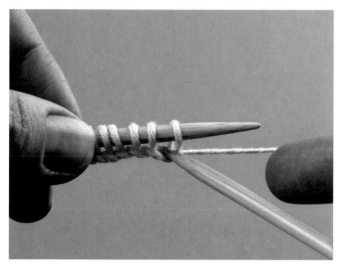

1 Place the right needle between the first and second stitches.

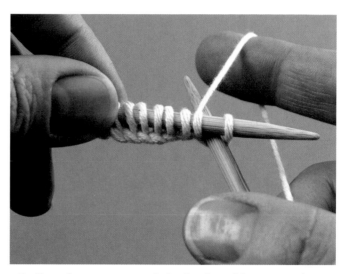

2 Pass the yarn around the back and between the two needles.

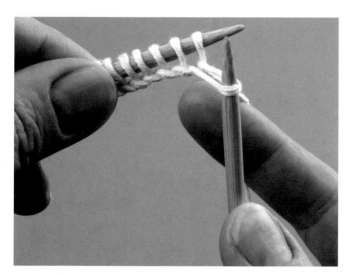

3 Pull the loop on the right hand needle towards you. Pass the yarn around the back and between the two needles.

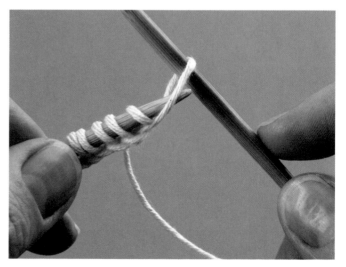

4 Place this new stitch with the other stitches on the left needle. Repeat until the required number of stitches is made.

Basic stitches
Most knitted fabrics are made up of one or two stitches—knit and purl. Working a knit row and then a purl row alternately produces stockinette stitch. With stockinette stitch, the knit side is the right side.

knit stitch
This is the basic knitting stitch. If you only made knit stitches you would end up with garter stitch.

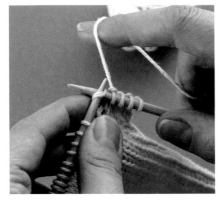 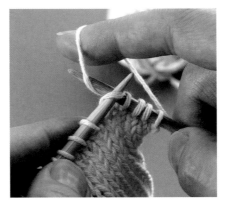 

1 Cast on the required stitches onto the left needle. Insert the point of the right needle from front to back through the first loop on the left needle.

2 Pass the yarn (which is always at the back of work for plain knitting) between the two needle points.

3 Draw the loop through to the front of the work. Pull the left needle under the right one, drawing the loop through with it.

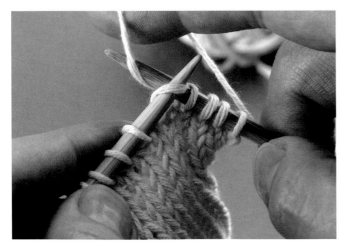 

4 Slip the remaining stitch off the left needle. Your stitch will now be on the right needle. Continue like this to the end of the row.

5 To knit the next row, turn your work around so the back is facing you and the stitches are on your left needle again. The empty needle is ready to receive the next row of stitches.

purl stitch

This is identical to the knit stitch, but is just done backwards. If you knitted all purl stitches, you would have garter stitch, just as if you had done only knit stitches.

1 Beginning with the yarn at the front, insert the right needle from back to front into the first stitch on the left needle.

2 Pass the yarn (which for purl is always held in front of your work) over and around the point of the right needle.

3 Draw the loop through to the back.

4 Slide the first stitch off the left needle. Continue like this to the end of the row.

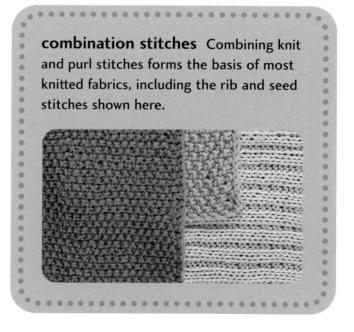

combination stitches Combining knit and purl stitches forms the basis of most knitted fabrics, including the rib and seed stitches shown here.

Shaping
Increasing or decreasing the number of stitches is how knitwear is shaped. Once you have mastered the art of shaping, you can knit any kind of garment or shape.

increasing
This can be done anywhere in a row, but it should always be done where specified in the pattern.

KNITTING INTO THE BACK OF A STITCH
Where the increase is made on the first or last stitch in a row, an extra stitch is created at the increase point. Knit the first stitch, but instead of dropping the stitch off the left needle, place the point of the right needle into the back of the stitch, knit it, and drop it off the left needle. You now have two stitches on the right needle. Work purl increases in the same way, but purlwise.

FULLY FASHIONED INCREASING
This is where the increase is made not on the first or last stitch but usually on the third stitch from the edge. It may also be made on the second stitch from the edge or across the work at regular points, if you want to widen your work suddenly as a feature.

The mark made when increasing in this way is called a fashioning mark, and this technique is often used as a design feature, particularly on finer knitwear or when using a smooth yarn such as mercerized cotton. This visible mark on your work is also useful for counting your increases.

1 On a knit row, knit the first two stitches.

2 Then knit the third stitch, but instead of dropping this stitch off the left needle, place the point of the right needle into the back of the stitch, knit this loop too, then drop the stitch off.

decreasing

This is the shaping that makes your work narrower. You do this by knitting or purling two stitches together to reduce them to one stitch.

SIMPLE DECREASING

Pass the tip of the right needle through the first two stitches on the left needle and work together, producing one stitch on the right needle. For purl rows, work as above but decrease purlwise.

FULLY FASHIONED DECREASING

This works two stitches together, but instead of knitting together the end two stitches, work together the second and third or third and fourth stitches to produce a fashioning mark on the right side of your work. This method will produce a slope from left to right. For purl rows, work as above but purlwise.

Sometimes a pattern uses decreases on both sides of a garment, and uses the marks as a design feature, then it is important that the stitches slope in the correct way.

To get a right-to-left slope on a knit row, at the decrease point, slip the first stitch (pass it to the other needle without knitting it), knit the next stitch, then pass the slipped stitch over the knitted stitch. To get a right-to-left slope on a purl row, purl the first stitch and then put it back onto the left needle, lift the next stitch over it, and then return it to the right needle.

Binding off
Always bind off in the appropriate stitch for your work—that is knitwise on a knit row and purlwise on a purl row. Binding off on a purl row will have less of a tendency to roll, and the edge is less visible from the right side. If binding off a rib, bind off in both knit and purl, following the rib pattern.

simple binding off
On a purl row, purl the first two stitches then bind off as described below, but purling every stitch. It is not necessary to bind off between every stitch. On a knit row, work as follows.

1 On a knit row, knit the first two stitches.

2 With the left needle, lift the first stitch over the second, then knit the second stitch (which is now the first on the needle). Follow this pattern of lifting one stitch over the next then knitting the next stitch until just one stitch remains. Break off the yarn and pass the tail through the last loop.

joining in a new color Always tie the ends together when joining a new color or fresh ball of yarn to your work. This will prevent a hole appearing due to unraveling ends. As you add a new color or fresh yarn, always leave long ends—they are useful for sewing up the seams of your work.

Repairing a dropped stitch
Try to repair a dropped stitch and correct your work from the right side. To repair a dropped stitch on the wrong side of your work, repair in the same way but with your stitch at the back of your work. If you are repairing a stitch in a patterned piece of work, make sure you knit or purl where appropriate.

1 Make sure that your stitch is at the front of your work and then use your knitting needle or a crochet hook to pick up the horizontal threads, pulling each thread through the stitch one at a time until you have picked up all the dropped stitches.

2 Place the stitch back on your needle.

Using a stitch marker

Wrap a contrasting piece of yarn around the stitch you wish to mark and tie in a double knot.

Alternatively, use bought plastic stitch markers, made for the purpose.

finishing your work

This section contains a variety of finishing techniques, including adding buttonholes and making a pom-pom. You will also find a variety of embroidery stitches to embellish your work, and some reliable methods to join pieces of work together.

Buttonholes
It is important to correctly position buttonholes—two or three stitches in from the edge of the work—because they create a gauge in your work. It is worth over-sewing your buttonhole to give it a firm edge, since with time wear on the threads on either side of the hole may cause the yarn to break and unravel. Simply work an overstitch or small blanket stitch around each buttonhole to protect the edge.

horizontal
This is the most common buttonhole to work. It is used where the strain on the buttonhole is from side to side.

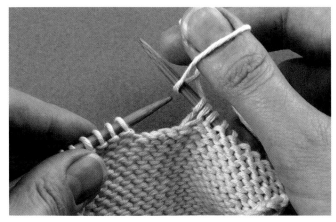

1 At the required position, and starting on a knit row, bind off the number of stitches required for the size of your button. On the return row, cast on over the bound-off stitches using the thumb method (see page 91), and work to the end of the row.

2 On the following rows, knit or purl the stitches according to your pattern, so that the number of stitches in the row is restored.

vertical

This buttonhole style is needed only where the strain on the button is up or down. It is very simple to do.

Simply divide your work in two to make a vertical slit. At the point where the buttonhole begins, keep the remaining stitches on a stitch holder and continue knitting the stitches on your needle until the buttonhole measures the required length. Place these stitches on a stitch holder and repeat the process on the opposite side. When the work is of the same length, continue on all the stitches together, so completing the buttonhole.

eyelet

This buttonhole is suitable for fine knitwear, and can also be used as a method for threading ribbon along the edges of your work.

1 Working on a knit row, when you come to the place to make the eyelet buttonhole, put the yarn forward over the needle.

2 Knit the next two stitches together. In the next row, the made stitch is purled in the usual way.

Cables
A cable pattern, which is usually worked on the knit row, gives an embossed effect to your knitting. There are numerous variations on cable patterns, some of which look very complicated but are worth attempting for their stunning results.

In addition to your yarn and knitting needles, you will need a cable needle (cn) or double-pointed needle (dpn) to work a cable. The cn holds the stitches so that the twist in your work can be made. Slip the first group of stitches in your cable onto the cn, then place this either at the front or back of your work (see below). Knit the number of stitches specified in the pattern, followed by the stitches from the cn.

Holding the stitches on the cn at the back of your work produces a cable that twists to the right, while holding the stitches on the cn at the front of your work gives a cable that twists to the left. If you are knitting two cables on either side of a textured panel, making one cable twist to the right and the other to the left will give your work a pleasing symmetry.

Most basic cables are crossed after you have worked the same number of rows as there are stitches in the cable width. By crossing the stitches after fewer rows have been worked, a more corded effect is achieved. To cross a basic four-stitch cable, work as follows.

1 Follow your pattern to the cable cross row, then work to the four stitches of the cable. There will usually be at least one purl stitch on either side of a cable, which helps the cable stand out. Put the next two stitches onto the cn.

2 Knit the next two stitches, then knit the two stitches from the cn.

3 Continue working in the pattern to the end.

Fair Isle

When knitting Fair Isle, you will usually have two colors on each row, and the colors not being used must be woven or stranded across the back of the work. There are two main techniques used for this: stranding and weaving in.

STRANDING

Stranding is where the yarn is left loose across the back of the work, but will never pass more than four or five stitches before being picked up and used again. Stranding is the traditional method used in the Shetland Islands, and is often preferred to weaving in because it keeps a softer, more pliable feel to the work. However, if these strands are pulled too tightly across the back of the work they can greatly distort the work and result in an uneven fabric.

WEAVING IN

Weaving in, by contrast, is where the yarn not being knitted is woven over and under the color in use. The color not in use is passed over the color in use when knitting one stitch, and under the color in use on the following stitch. This creates a thicker fabric without the floating threads at the back of the work. Use the weaving method if a color is left unused for more than four or five stitches, or for sleeves and other areas where fingers can get caught in the strands.

The back of the work in this sample shows stranding across several stitches.

The pattern at the front of the work should be even and flat. If the threads are pulled unevenly at the back of the work it will gather the fabric.

To weave in, twist the threads together at the back of each stitch so as not to leave long running threads.

Crochet edging
One of the best ways to employ crochet is to produce neat and decorative edgings. Here is one of the simplest techniques—try working it with different yarns and ribbons to achieve different finishes.

reverse single crochet or corded edging

Join yarn to edge of work. Begin by working one row of sc evenly along the edge of work, being careful not to pull the work too tightly. Work back along the row in sc, without turning work, from left to right.

Making a tie cord
This simple technique can include more than one color of yarn to make a jazzy, multicolored cord that will complement the finished knitwear.

1 Measure a piece of thread eight times as long as the cord length required. Fold it in half, then in half again (4 ends together). Hold it firmly at one end then twist the other end very tightly in a clockwise direction. The tighter the twist, the better the cord will be.

2 Fold it in half again, and the cord will twist together. Tie a knot at one end.

Making a pom-pom
Pom-poms are fun to make, and provide great embellishments for your knitting—try using different fibers for added texture and sparkle.

1 Cut 2 circles of card to whatever diameter of pom-pom you require, and cut a circular hole in the center approximately 1¼" (3 cm) in diameter (or smaller for finer yarn). Alternatively, you can use a readymade pom-pom maker, as shown.

2 Put the two pieces of card together and wrap the yarn around them, threading it through the hole in the center. Cover the whole shape with yarn. The more yarn you use and the closer together you wrap the yarn, the fuller your pom-pom will be.

3 With a sharp pair of scissors, cut the threads all around the circle on the outside edge between the two pieces of card.

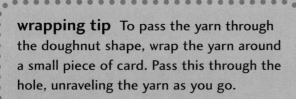

wrapping tip To pass the yarn through the doughnut shape, wrap the yarn around a small piece of card. Pass this through the hole, unraveling the yarn as you go.

4 Ease the pieces of card apart so that you can reach the center. Wrap a piece of yarn around the center, and tie it in a tight and secure knot. Leave long ends on the knot, and use these to attach the pom-pom to your main work. Cut away and remove the card. Fluff up the pom-pom, trimming the ends if necessary for a neat finish.

Embroidery
As you become more confident, you may wish to personalize your work. Use these stitches to embelish the areas of your work once the garment is finished.

chain stitch

Draw a needle through the fabric from back to front, then reinsert the needle just to the right of where it came through, holding some of the thread down to create a small loop. Take a stitch of the required length, making sure the needle passes up through the loop to form the first "chain" link. Repeat, shaping the chain stitches around your work as required.

> **fashion tip** Use chain stitch to embroider lines like flower stems, or letters. Use blanket stitch to finish edges of fabric.

blanket stitch

1 Working from left to right, bring a darning needle, or blunt ended knitter's needle, threaded with yarn through the knitting where you want the top of the stitch to be.

2 Hold the thread down, and insert the needle to the right. Pass the needle through the loop, as shown. Pull the needle through until the thread forms a horizontal bar, and continue working to the right.

Preparation for finishing
Different weights of garment will require different preparations before being sewn up. Generally, the heavier the fabric, the less need there is for pulling the individual pieces into place using blocking or steaming before sewing up.

blocking

This simply means pinning out the knitted pieces on a flat surface (usually a blanket or towel covered in cotton) and making sure the measurements are correct. It also enables you to pull all the stitches in to place if needed.

Pin all around the work, sticking the pins in vertically through the garment at ¾" (2 cm) intervals into the soft surface below. Do not block any ribbing that is on a garment: this should be left loose.

> **stopping knitting** Always work to the end of a row before you stop knitting. If you finish in the middle of a row, you may find that a loop appears when you continue, because the work has stretched. In addition, you may lose your place in the row and this will muddle your pattern.

steaming

Never iron directly on your work, as it may burn or distort it, and it is hard to get a garment back to the correct shape once it has been damaged. As an alternative to pressing pieces before finishing, you can sew the garment together first, and then steam the finished piece with strong gusts of steam from an iron.

Using a damp cloth with a hot, dry iron instead of using a steam iron is also very effective, but you must keep the cloth damp at all times. Have a bowl of water beside you as you iron, so that you can dip the cloth into it to redampen it. Place the damp cloth onto the garment and press with the hot iron.

Joining seams
Having checked your pieces and prepared them (if necessary), you are now ready for the final stages of tidying up any ends and sewing the seams. If you have used contrast colors and the yarn has met midrow, weave the ends along the meeting point of the two colors. Never sew in ends across your work, as they will show and tend to pop through to the right side.

mattress stitch

The best way to sew side seams together is using mattress stitch. It creates a wonderful flat seam that is strong and versatile and quick to do; and, if done well, it should be invisible.

1 Arrange the two pieces to be joined side by side, with their right sides facing you. Insert a threaded darning needle into the edge of one of the pieces from front to back, following a vertical line between the end and second to end stitch. Bring the needle up after two rows then pass the needle to the opposite side and repeat.

2 Continue in this way, pulling the edges together and being careful to follow the same vertical line.

finishing tip Weave in any loose ends securely, so that you do not leave threads dangling inside a garment.

backstitch

Use backstitch for the shoulder seams. This is a quick and firm stitch, which most people know how to do. It is done with right sides together.

edge-to-edge stitch

There is also an edge-to-edge method that will form an almost invisible seam and will avoid any bulk or hardness at shoulder seam-type edges. With right sides facing you, insert a threaded darning needle from below into the end stitch. Pull the thread through then insert the needle into the matching stitch on the opposite piece and pass through two loops, coming out onto the right side. Insert the needle back into the original stitch where the thread first appeared. This has the effect of a stitch that is sewn, not knitted.

joining work with a crochet hook

Once you have mastered crochet, this is a quick and neat way to join particularly long seams. Using a small hook, the same size of the knitting needles used or smaller, run a slip stitch along the selvage edge, picking up the loose threads between the stitches.

Once the seams have been sewn, sew in any loose yarn ends by weaving them vertically into the seams. This can also be done with a crochet hook.

Useful information

Wouldn't it be great if everyone used the same terms to write about yarns and needles? Unfortunately, sizes are often based on metric or imperial measurements, or are based on arbitrary systems of numbers and letters. If in doubt, use a needle gauge to find the millimeter measurement.

On these pages you will find some conversion charts that will help you to convert needles and yarns into the standard sizes that are used in the patterns.

These charts are based on the recommendations of the Craft Yarn Council of America. You can see further information on their website, www.yarnstandards.com.

yarn weights

If you are going to use a different fiber than the one recommended, it is crucial that you do a gauge swatch to ensure that you can match the gauge given at the beginning of each pattern, otherwise your knitwear will not match the finished measurements supplied.

Use the chart below as a guide to help find the right gauge for your new wool, and to choose which weight of yarn to buy to match the symbol given with each pattern.

YARN WEIGHT SYMBOL GIVEN IN THE PATTERN	1	2	3	4	5	6
TYPES OF YARNS IN CATEGORY	Sock, fingering, baby	Sport, baby	Double knitting, light worsted	Worsted, afghan, Aran	Chunky, craft, rug	Bulky, roving
KNIT GAUGE RANGE IN STOCKINETTE STITCH TO 4" (10 CM)	27–32 sts	23–26 sts	21–24 sts	16–20 sts	12–15 sts	6–11 sts
RECOMMENDED NEEDLE SIZE IN METRIC RANGE	2.25–3.25 mm	3.25–4.5 mm	3.75–4.5 mm	4.5–5.5 mm	5.5–8 mm	8 mm and larger
RECOMMENDED NEEDLE SIZE	1 to 3	3 to 5	5 to 7	7 to 9	9 to 11	11 and larger
CROCHET GAUGE IN SINGLE CROCHET TO 4" (10 CM)	21–32 sts	16–20 sts	12–17 sts	11–14 sts	8–11 sts	5–9 sts
RECOMMENDED HOOK IN METRIC RANGE	2.25–3.5 mm	3.5–4.5 mm	4.5–5.5 mm	5.5–6.5 mm	6.5–9 mm	9 mm and larger
RECOMMENDED HOOK RANGE	B-1 to E-4	E-4 to 7	7 to I-9	I-9 to K-10½	K-10½ to M/N-13	M/N-13 and larger

abbreviations

Looking at a knitting pattern for the first time can feel like reading a foreign language. The shortened words are used to prevent laborious repetition, and to make the patterns shorter and easier to follow. Special abbreviations used are mentioned in the Stitch Glossary at the start of individual patterns. The following abbreviations are common to knitting patterns, and are used throughout the book.

KNITTING NEEDLES SIZES	
USA Size	Millimeters
0	2
1	2.25
--	2.5
2	2.75
--	3
3	3.25
4	3.5
5	3.75
6	4
7	4.5
8	5
9	5.5
10	6
10.5	6.5
--	7
--	7.5
11	8
13	9
15	10

CROCHET HOOK SIZES	
USA Size	Millimeters
B-1	2.25
C-2	2.75
D-3	3.25
E-4	3.5
F-5	3.75
G-6	4
7	4.5
H-8	5
I-9	5.5
J-10	6
K-10½	6.5
L-11	8
M/N-13	9
N/P-15	10
P/Q	15
Q	16
S	19

[]	work instructions within brackets as many times as directed
()	work instructions within parentheses in the place directed
**	repeat instructions following the asterisks as directed
*	repeat instructions following the single asterisk as directed
"	inch(es)
alt	alternate
approx	approximately
beg	begin/beginning
bet	between
BO	bind off
C2R	cable 2 right
CC	contrasting color
cm	centimetres
cn	cable needle
CO	cast on
cont	continue
dec	decrease
dpn	double pointed needle(s)
Fl	front loops
foll	follow/follows/following
g	gram
inc	increase
k or K	knit
k2tog	knit two stitches together

kwise	knitwise
LH	left hand
LPC	left purl cross
lp(s)	loop(s)
m	meters
M1	make one—an increase
M1 p-st	make one purl stitch
MC	main color
mm	millimetre(s)
oz	ounce(s)
p or P	purl
pat	pattern
pm	place marker
p2tog	purl 2 stitches together
prev	previous
psso	pass slipped stitch over
pwise	purlwise
rem	remaining
rep	repeat(s)
rev st st	reverse stockinette stitch
RH	right hand
rnd(s)	round(s)
RC	right cross
RPC	right purl cross
RS	right side
sk	skip
sk2p	slip1, knit 2 together, pass slip stitch over the knit 2 together; 2 stitches have been decreased

skp	slip, knit, pass stitch over— one stitch decreased
sl	slip
sl1k	slip 1 knitwise
sl1p	slip 1 purlwise
ss	slip stitch(es)
ssk	slip, slip, knit slipped stitches together
st(s)	stitches
St st	stockinette stitch
tbl	through back loop
tog	together
WS	wrong side
w&t	wrap and turn
wyib	with yarn in back
wyif	with yarn in front
yd(s)	yard(s)
yfwd	yarn forward
yo	yarn over
yrn	yarn around needle
yon	yarn over needle

CROCHET ABBREVIATIONS

ch	chain
dc	double crochet
hdc	half double crochet
sc	single crochet
Sl st	slip stitch
tr	treble

Acknowledgments

Many thanks to BJ Berti, Claretta Bostic-Holland, Lisa Buccellato, Victoria Hilditch, Joyce Nordstrom, Fran Scullin, Shirley Rinehart, and Judy Timmer.

Sources for supplies

Contact the companies listed below for purchasing and mail-order information.

yarn

Bernat Yarns
320 Livingston Avenue South, Listowel, ON, Canada N4W 3H3, 1-800-265-2864
www.bernatyarns.com

Berroco
14 Emdale Road, Uxbridge, MA 01569
www.berroco.com

Brown Sheep Co.
100662 Country Road 16, Mitchell, NE 69357
www.brownsheep.com

Cascade Yarns
1224 Andover Park East, Tukwila, WA 98188
www.cascadeyarns.com

Classic Elite Yarns
122 Western Avenue, Lowell, MA 01851
www.classiceliteyarns.com

Coats & Clark/Red Heart
PO Box 12229, Greenville, SC 29612-0229
www.coatsandclark.com

JCA Crafts Inc./Reynolds
35 Scales Lane, Townsend MA 01469-1094
www.jcacrafts.com

Lion Brand Yarn
135 Kero Road., Carlstdt, NJ 07072
www.lionbrand.com

Patons
320 Livingstone Avenue South, Listowel, ON, Canada, N4W 3H3
www.patonsyarns.com

Plymouth Yarn Company
PO Box 28, Bristol, PA 19007
www.plymouthyarn.com

Skacel Collection
PO Box 88110, Seattle, WA 98138-2110
www.skacelknitting.com

Tahki/Stacy Charles Inc.
70–30 80th St., Building 36, Ridgewood, NY 11385
www.tahkistacycharles.com

Westminster Fibers Inc./Rowan Yarn
4 Townsend West, Unit 8, Nashua, NH 03063
www.knitrowan.com

ribbon

Mokuba New York
55 W.39th St
New York,
NY 10019, 212 869 8900